GIFTED & TALENTED®

To develop your child's gifts and talents

ANIMALS

A Science Workbook for Ages 4–6

Written by Mary Kraynak Bozansky, M.S., and Bailey Kennedy, M.S.

Illustrated by Dave Lowe

McGraw-Hill Children's Publishing

Columbus, Ohio

*Reviewed and endorsed by Barbara Saffer, Ph.D., who holds
degrees in biology and geology and has taught many college-level
science courses. Her science articles and puzzles have appeared in*
Cricket, Scholastic Dynamath, Nature Friend, *and
several other magazines for children.*

*McGraw-Hill
Children's Publishing*
A Division of The **McGraw·Hill** Companies

Copyright © 2003 McGraw-Hill Children's Publishing.

All rights reserved. Except as permitted under the United States Copyright Act, no part of this publication may be reproduced or distributed in any form or by any means, or stored in a database retrieval system, without prior written permission from the publisher.

Send all inquiries to:
McGraw-Hill Children's Publishing
8787 Orion Place
Columbus, Ohio 43240-4027

ISBN 1-56565-746-2

Printed in China.

1 2 3 4 5 6 7 8 9 10 STR 06 05 04 03 02

Note to Parents

GIFTED & TALENTED® WORKBOOKS will help develop your child's natural talents and gifts by providing activities to enhance critical and creative thinking skills. These skills of logic and reasoning teach children **how** to think. They are precisely the skills emphasized by teachers of gifted and talented children.

Thinking skills are the skills needed to be able to learn anything at any time. Unlike events, words, and teaching methods, thinking skills never change. If a child has a grasp of how to think, school success and even success in life will become more assured. In addition, the child will become self-confident as he or she approaches new tasks with the ability to think them through and discover solutions.

GIFTED & TALENTED® WORKBOOKS present these skills in a unique way, combining the basic subject areas of reading, language arts, math, and science with thinking skills. The top of each page is labeled to indicate the specific thinking skill being developed. Here are some of the skills you will find:

- Comprehension—the ability to understand concepts put into sentences
- Creative Thinking—the ability to generate unique ideas; to compare and contrast the same elements in different situations; to discover imaginative solutions to problems
- Deduction—the ability to reach a logical conclusion by interpreting clues
- Inference—the ability to reach logical conclusions from given or assumed evidence
- Understanding Relationships—the ability to understand how objects, shapes, and words are similar or dissimilar; to classify and categorize

How to Use GIFTED & TALENTED® SCIENCE WORKBOOKS

Each book in this series contains activities that challenge children. The activities vary in range from easier to more difficult. You may need to work with your child on many of the pages, especially with the child who is a nonreader. However, even a nonreader can master thinking skills, and the sooner your child learns how to think, the better.

Read the directions to your child and, if necessary, explain them. Note that the words printed in bold face are listed in the glossary at the back of the book for your reference. The activities should be done consecutively, as the activity on each page builds upon the skills and information presented on the pages that precede it. When your child's interest wanes, stop. A page or two at a time may be enough, as the child should have fun while learning.

The included poster is an extra learning tool that you and your child can use together. Hang the poster in a very visible place. Then whenever you get the chance, talk about the various items pictured on the poster. Ask your child questions about the poster. What additional information can he or she tell you about the pictures?

It is important to remember that these activities are designed to teach your child **how to think,** not how to find the right answer. Teachers of gifted children are never surprised when a child discovers a new "right" answer. For example, a child may be asked to choose the object that doesn't belong in this group: a table, a chair, a book, a desk. The best answer is **book,** since all the others are furniture. But a child could respond that all of them belong because they all could be found in an office. The best way to react to this type of response is to praise the child and gently point out that there is another answer, too. While creativity should be encouraged, your child must look for the best and most **suitable** answer.

GIFTED & TALENTED® WORKBOOKS have been written and endorsed by educators. This series will benefit any child who demonstrates curiosity, imagination, a sense of fun and wonder about the world, and a desire to learn. These books will open your child's mind to new experiences and help fulfill his or her true potential.

Understanding Relationships/Deduction

There are many different living things in our world. Some living things are animals. Some living things are plants.

Draw a square around the animals. Draw a triangle around the plants.

Circle the correct number in each of the sentences below.

There are   2   4   6   animals on this page.

There are   3   5   7   plants on this page.

Many kinds of animals live in our world.

Circle the correct number in each sentence below.

There are   2   3   4   animals on this page that are **birds**.

There are   2   3   4   animals on this page that are **reptiles**.

There are   2   3   4   animals on this page that are **fish**.

There are   2   3   4   animals on this page that are **mammals**.

Do you know that there are other kinds of animals as well? Can you name them? _____

_____

Visual Discrimination/Understanding Relationships

People in a family are alike in important ways. They may walk or talk in the same way. They may look alike.

Animals in a family are alike in important ways, too.

Draw a line from each animal to its family. Then, next to each family name, write the number of animals on this page that belong to it.

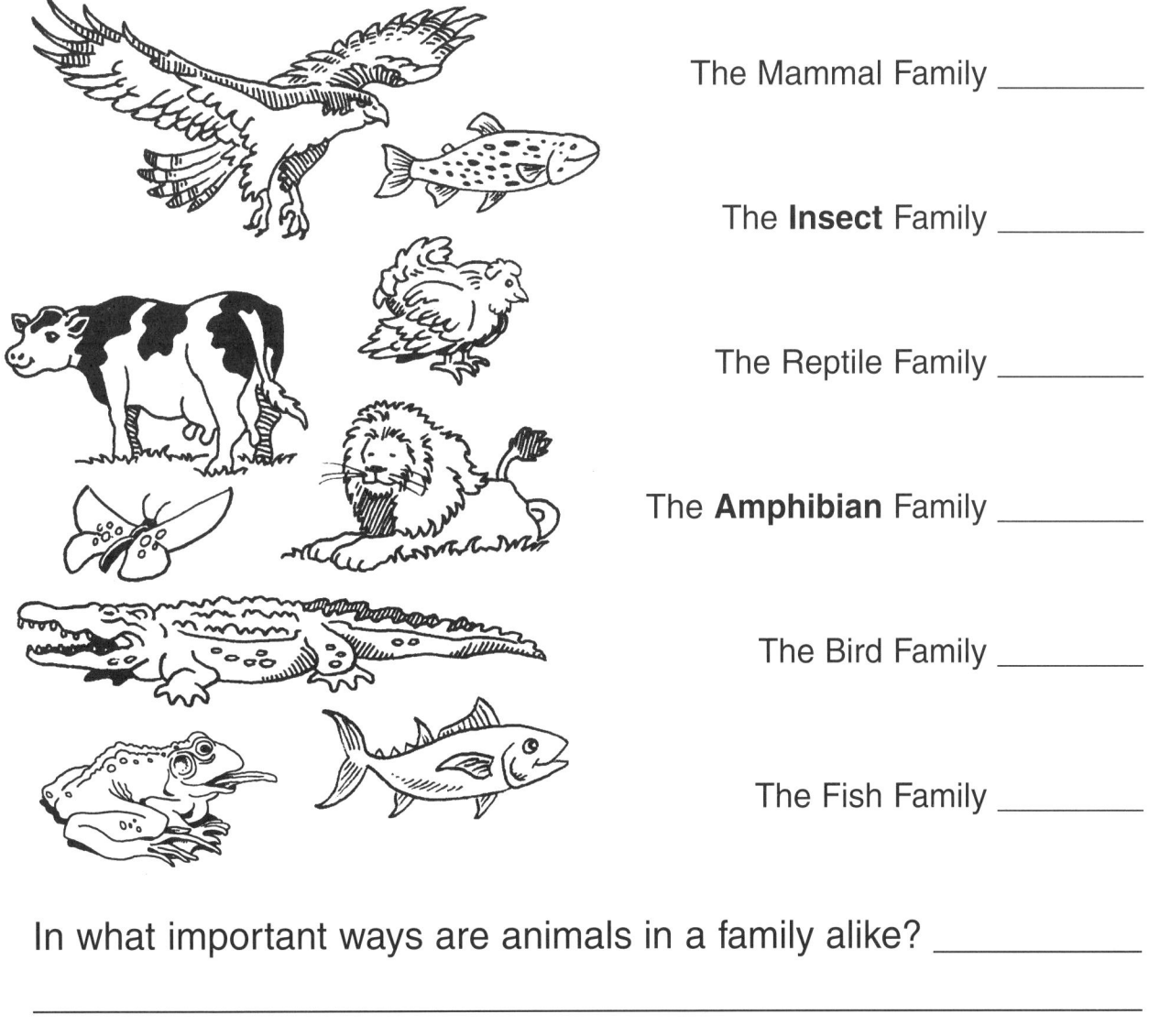

The Mammal Family _____

The **Insect** Family _____

The Reptile Family _____

The **Amphibian** Family _____

The Bird Family _____

The Fish Family _____

In what important ways are animals in a family alike? _____

7

Visual Discrimination/Understanding Relationships

Animals in the bird family are alike in many important ways. Can you see the ways in the pictures below?

Look at the pictures. Circle one animal in each row that belongs to the bird family.

Circle the correct number in each sentence below.

All birds have   2   3   4   wings.

All birds have   2   3   4   legs.

What else makes the birds above alike? _____

_____

Visual Discrimination/Inference

All birds have 2 legs for walking. Some birds have short legs. Some birds have long legs.

Draw a square around the birds with long legs. How many of these birds do you see? _____

Use crayons to color all the birds that have short legs. How many of these birds did you color? _____

Do all the birds have the same kind of feet? _____

Do all the birds have **claws** on their feet? _____

Analogies/Understanding Relationships

The kind of feet a bird has depends on how the bird lives.

Swimming birds, like ducks, have **webbed feet** to help them swim. Skin between the toes helps them to use their feet as paddles.

Wading birds, like herons, have long legs and long toes to help them wade in the water as they look for fish or tadpoles to eat.

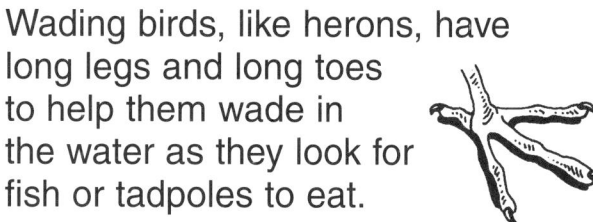

Ground birds, like chickens, have scratching feet for digging and finding food in the ground

Meat-eating birds, like owls, have long, sharp claws on their feet that they use to catch small animals to eat.

Birds that climb trees, like woodpeckers, have two toes pointing backward and two toes pointing forward so they can hold on to the sides of trees.

Circle the foot that best completes each sentence.

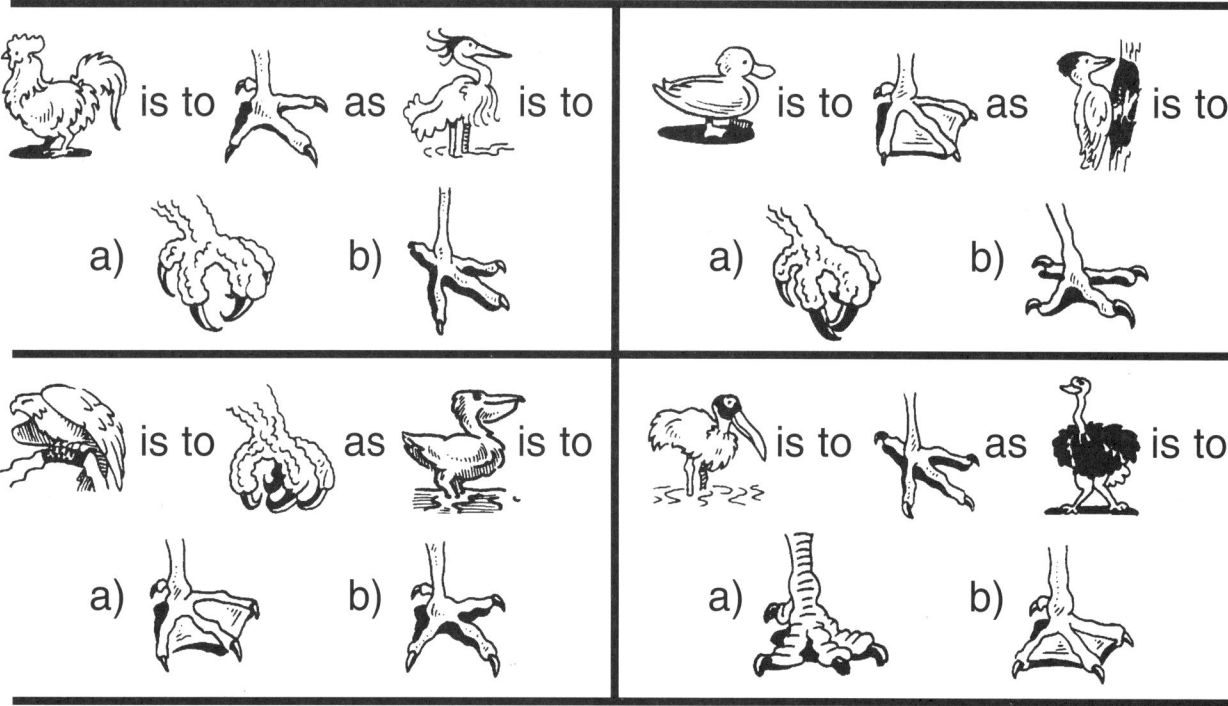

Most birds have 4 toes on each foot. How many toes do you have on each foot? _____

Analogies/Understanding Relationships/Recall

The kind of **beak,** also called a **bill,** that a bird has depends on what it eats.

Birds with short, strong beaks, like sparrows, use their bills to crack open seeds and nuts to eat.

Birds with long, thin beaks, like woodpeckers, use their bills to catch insects to eat.

Birds with spearlike beaks, like cranes, use their bills to scoop up fish to eat.

Birds with hooked beaks, like eagles, use their bills to tear apart small animals to eat.

A hummingbird uses its long, thin beak to suck juicy nectar from flowers.

Circle the beak that best completes each sentence.

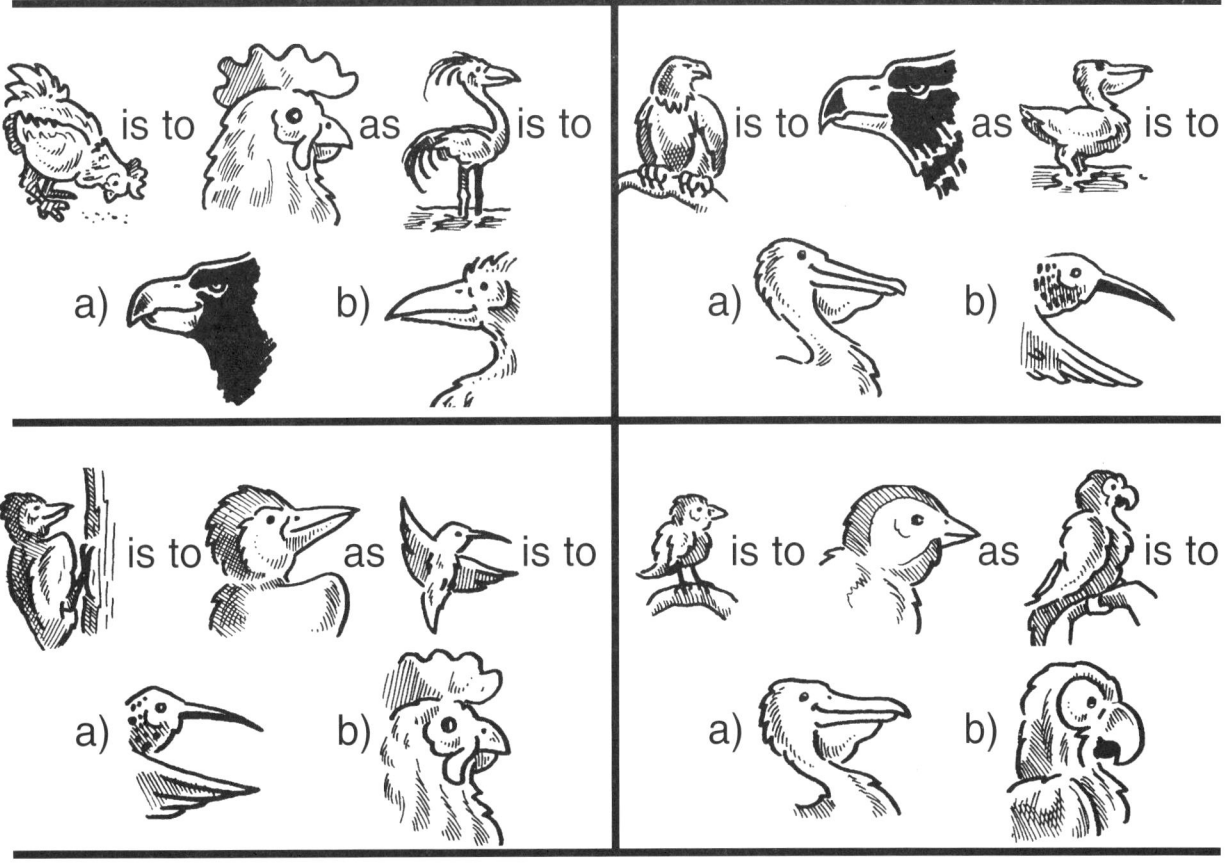

Deduction

Most birds can fly, but some birds cannot fly. A penguin and an ostrich cannot fly. An emu cannot fly, either. A chicken can fly only **very** short distances.

Circle three birds in each row that can fly long distances.

How many birds did you circle altogether? _____

Creative Thinking/Deduction

Why do you think birds like penguins, ostriches, and emus cannot fly? **Hint:** Think about the parts of a bird's body that help it fly. How are those parts different on birds that can fly and birds that cannot fly? _____
_____

All birds have **wings** and feathers. But the wings of birds like penguins, ostriches, and emus are not strong enough to hold the birds up in the air to fly.

Penguins are water birds that can swim very fast. Baby penguins like to use their bellies to slide on the snow and ice! Do you think a penguin has webbed feet or clawed feet? _____
Why? _____
_____

The ostrich is the biggest bird in the world. It can grow to be taller than a very tall human. It can run very fast. What kind of legs do you think an ostrich has? _____
Why? _____
_____

Creative Thinking/Deduction

Help this bird walk. Draw the bird's toes, and then draw its claws. Why does this bird need claws? _____
_____
_____

Help this bird eat. Draw the bird's beak. What kind of a beak will you draw? Why?
_____
_____

What can you add to this picture to help this bird fly? Draw your answer on the bird.

Understanding Relationships/Inference

Draw a line from each bird to the box that contains at least three of its body parts. Then put an **X** on the body part in that box that does **not** belong to that bird.

What body part did you put an **X** on in each box? _____

Deduction/Recall

> I am a bird.
> I have sharp claws for catching small animals to eat.
> I have a hooked beak.
> I stay awake at night.
> What am I? _____

Color me. I have brown and white feathers.

Why do you think I have big eyes? _____
_____

Creative Thinking/Inference

Goofy Birds!

What is wrong with these birds? Point to the body part that is wrong on each bird pictured below. Then write the letter that stands for the beginning sound of each of these incorrect body parts.

17

Analogies/Understanding Relationships

Birds usually live in **nests** that they build in protected places. Most birds build nests in trees. Eagles and hawks are different. They build their nests on high cliffs. Pelicans and penguins build their nests on the ground near water.

Circle the picture that best completes each sentence below.

Why do birds build nests? _____

Comprehension/Creative Thinking

Birds build nests so they have a safe place to lay their eggs and protect their newborn babies.

In most bird families, both the mother and father bird build the nest together. The mother bird then lays the eggs in the nest. Draw a mother and father bird building their nest in the box at the right.

The father bird often brings food to the mother bird. It will also help the mother bird by sitting on the eggs. Draw a father bird bringing food to a mother bird in the box at the left.

When the eggs hatch, both parents teach the baby birds how to fly and find food. Draw two baby birds standing on the edge of their nest, ready to fly, in the box at the right.

What are most nests made of? _____

_____

_____

Comprehension/Visual Discrimination

Birds build nests from all kinds of things. Look at the nests below.

Flamingos use mud to build nests in shallow water. Draw a circle around the flamingo's nest.

Orioles build hanging nests with grass, plant fibers, bark, and string. Draw a triangle around the oriole's nest.

Swallows build nests with mud and feathers in man-made structures like barns. Draw a diamond around the swallow's nest.

Swans build nests made of grass and reeds near the edge of water. Draw a rectangle around the swan's nest.

Say out loud each thing these birds use to build their nests.

Analogies/Understanding Relationships

Mother birds lay eggs that have a hard **shell**. Ducks, chickens, and swans are covered with feathers when they hatch from their eggs. Other birds hatch blind and naked. They need much more care and feeding by their parents.

Circle the picture that best completes each sentence below.

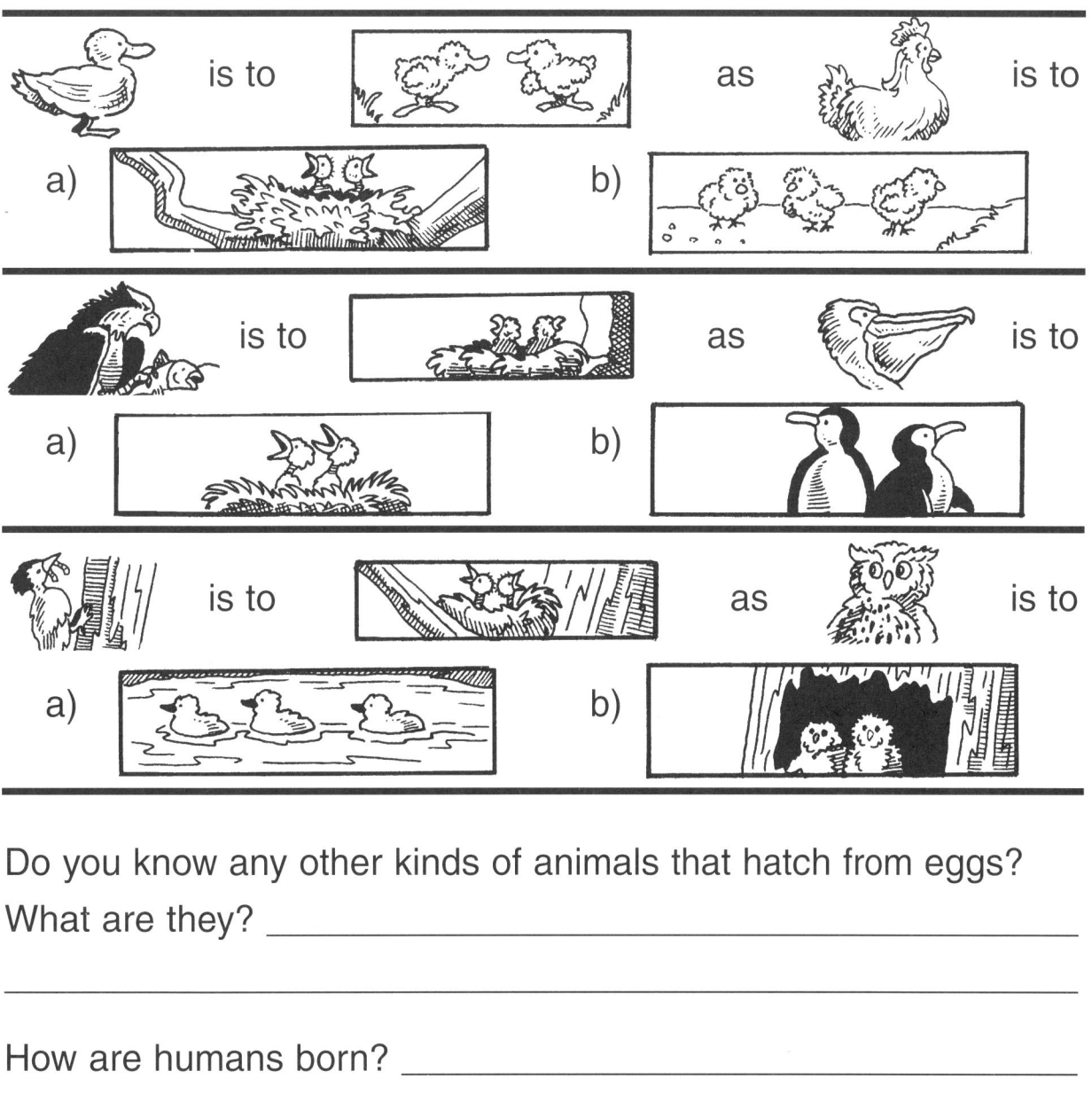

Do you know any other kinds of animals that hatch from eggs? What are they? _____

_____

How are humans born? _____

_____

21

Deduction/Understanding Relationships

Animals in the bird family are alike in important ways. Animals in the reptile family are alike in important ways, too.

Circle one animal in each row that belongs to the reptile family.

Do reptiles have smooth or scaly skin? _____

Do all reptiles have legs? _____

Creative Thinking/Inference

Most reptiles have 4 legs. Usually each foot has 5 toes with claws for digging.

Help these reptiles crawl. Draw their legs, toes, and claws.

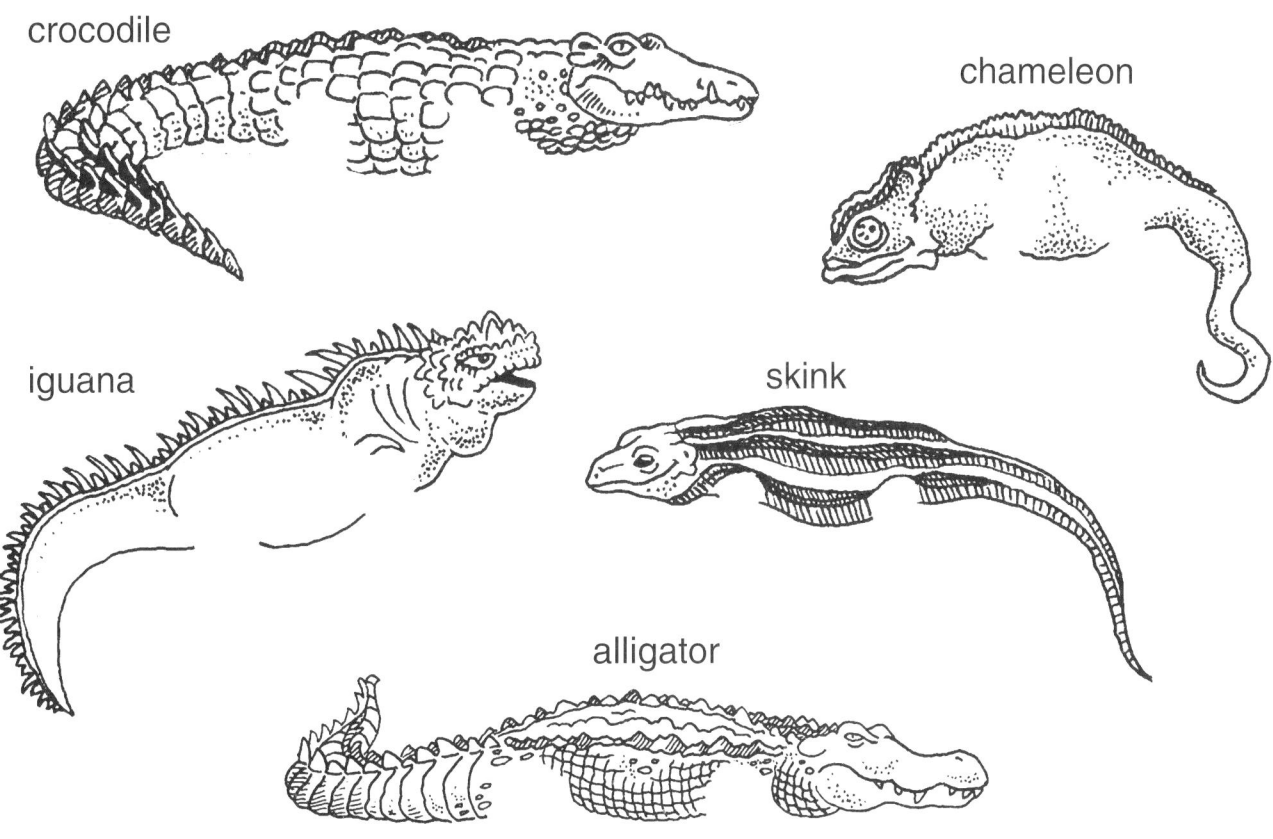

Which two reptiles above look very much alike? Circle them. Now write the letter that stands for the beginning sound in each of their names. _____   _____

In what other ways do you think reptiles are alike? _____
_____
_____

Turn the page to see if you are right.

Comprehension/Inference

All reptiles have **lungs** for breathing, a backbone, and scales or bony plates on the outside of their bodies. All reptiles are **cold-blooded** animals. This means their bodies are the same temperature as the water or air around them.

If a reptile is cold, it will **bask** in the sun. What do you think this means? _____

If a reptile is too hot, what do you think it will do? _____
_____

A snake is a reptile that has no legs. A snake can move very fast by wriggling its body along the ground. It can leave a mark like this:

Draw the slinky, slithering snake print that this snake has left behind.

Some snakes even climb trees and move from branch to branch. The scales and muscles on the undersides of their bodies help them move.

Snakes can open their mouths very wide. This helps them swallow food, like rats or birds, that are bigger than their mouths are.

As snakes grow bigger, they **shed,** or get rid of, their old skin. Why do you think they do this? _____
_____
_____

Comprehension/Creative Thinking

Turtles are slow-moving reptiles that have a heavy shell  made of bone and covered with bony plates. Most turtles can pull their legs, tail, and head inside their shell. They do this to help protect themselves.

Some turtles, like snapping turtles, live in water. They have webbed feet to help them swim. What other animals have webbed feet?

Some turtles, like box turtles, live on land. Their feet have small toes and claws to help them move over the ground.

Draw a pattern on this turtle's shell. Draw its legs and tail. Now decide where it lives—in the water or on land. Add the right kind of feet to its legs.

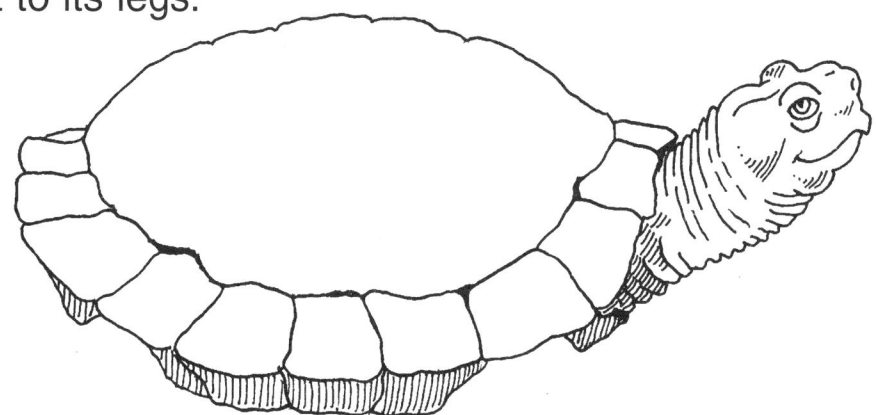

Now tell a story about this turtle to a friend or a family member.

Most mother reptiles lay eggs in a nest of dead plants or in shallow holes in the ground. Other mother reptiles carry their babies inside them until they are ready to be born.

Baby turtles, alligators, crocodiles, and some lizards hatch from eggs. Rattlesnakes and garter snakes come out of their mothers alive. Draw a line from each reptile below to its young **offspring**.

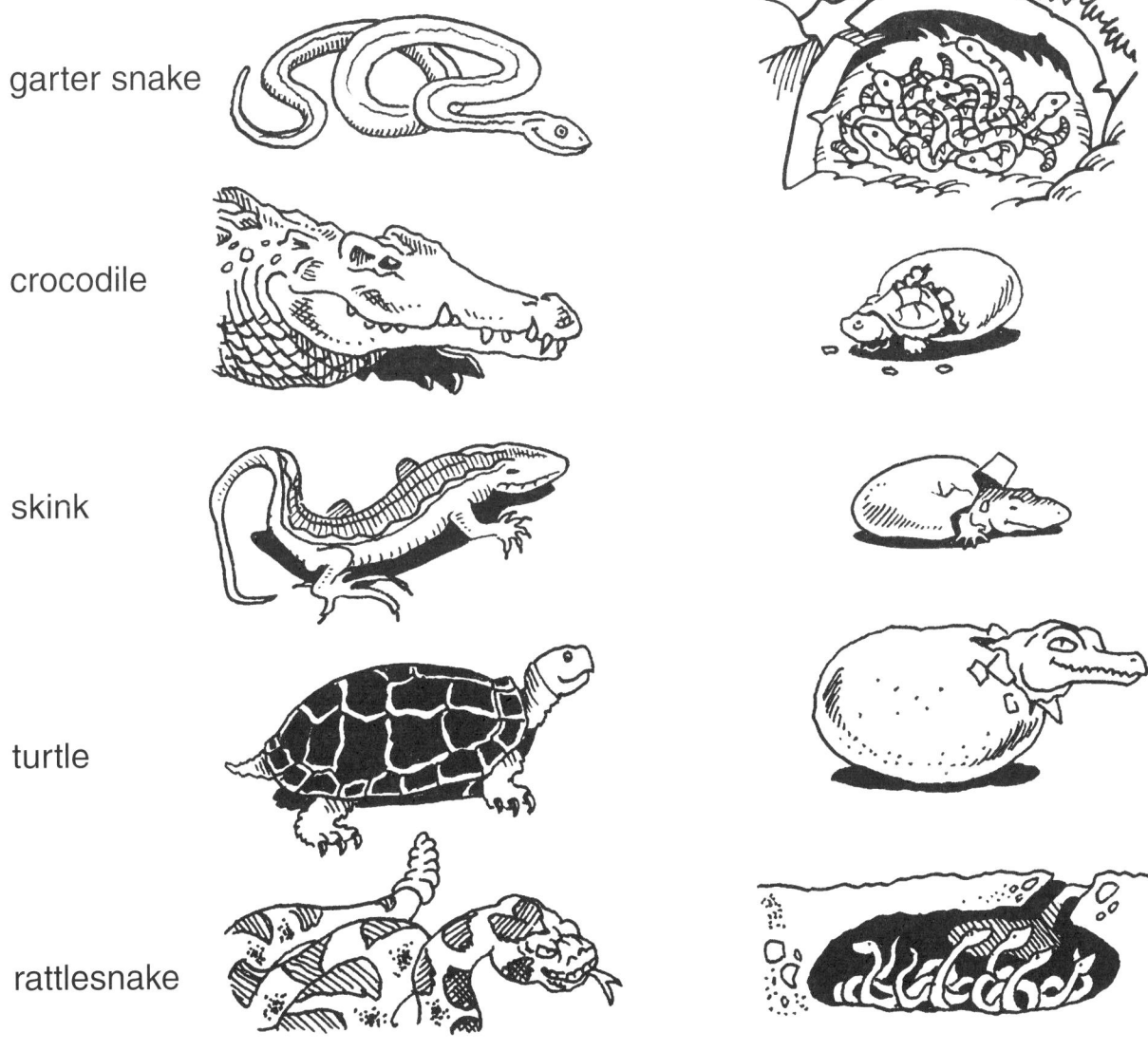

How many of the reptiles above are hatched from eggs? _____

Deduction/Understanding Relationships

Another animal family is the fish family. Animals in the fish family are alike in important ways.

Circle one animal in each row that belongs to the fish family.

How is a fish's skin different from a reptile's skin? _____

Do fish have legs? _____

Comprehension/Inference

All fish have fins for swimming in water. All fish have **gills** for breathing. Most fish have coats of slimy scales that cover their bodies.

Many fish, such as tuna, shark, and sea horses, live in salty oceans. Other fish, such as trout, catfish, and perch, live in freshwater rivers and lakes.

Draw a circle around the fish that do **not** live in salt water. Where do these fish live? _____

How many fish do you see that live in salt water? _____

Circle the correct number in each sentence below.
    On this page,   3   6   9   fish have fins for swimming.
    On this page,   2   4   6   fish have gills for breathing in water.

Creative Thinking/Inference

Help these fish swim in water by drawing fins on their bodies.

Give this fish a tail fin.

Give this fish a fin on top of its back.

Give this fish fins on the underside of its body.

Give this fish a fin on the side of its body.

Visual Discrimination/Deduction/Inference

Some fish have very large fins. Draw a rectangle around the fish with the largest fins. This fish looks like it flies through the water.

Does this fish have a tail? _____

Does it look like the other fish on this page? _____
Why or why not? _____
_____

Visual Discrimination/Inference/Understanding Relationships

Fish come in different shapes. Most fast-swimming fish have long, thin bodies to help them move quickly through the water. Put an **X** on the fish that does **not** have a slim, streamlined body.

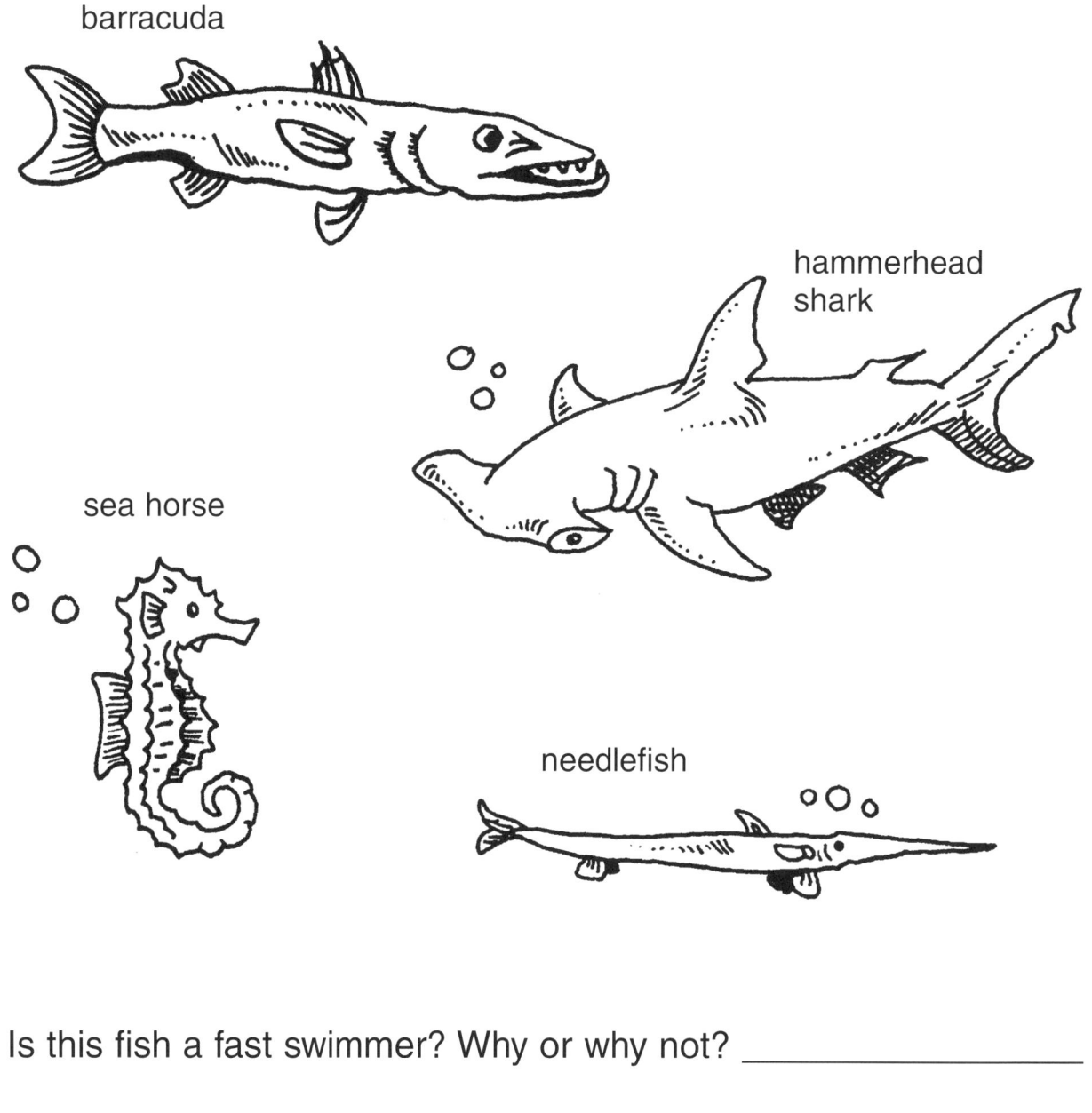

Is this fish a fast swimmer? Why or why not? _____

_____

How do you think this fish got its name? _____

_____

Inference/Visual Discrimination

Fish come in different colors. Ocean fish are often silvery blue. River fish are often brown. Fish that live in coral reefs are usually brightly colored.

Use a crayon to draw yellow and blue stripes on the butterfly fish. Where does the butterfly fish live? _____

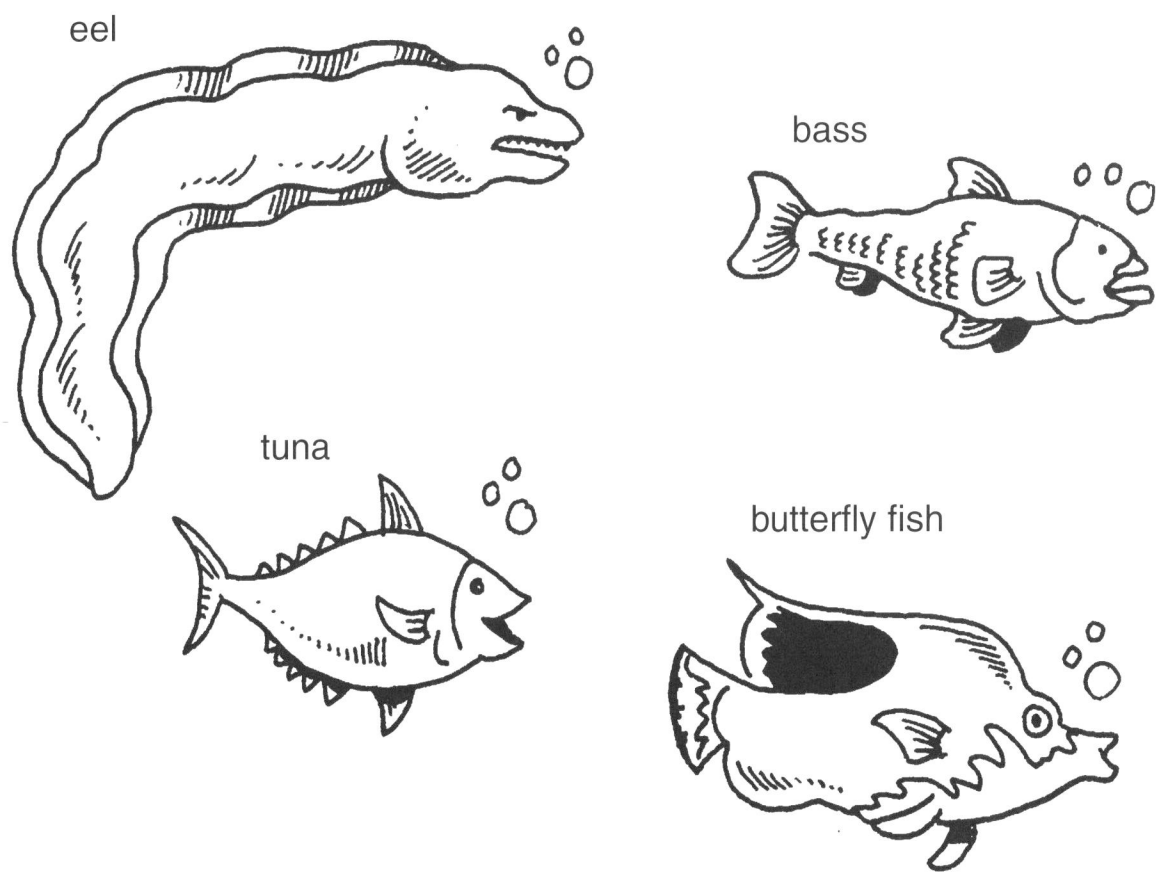

The tuna is an ocean fish just like most eels are. What color will you make this fish? Color it with crayons.

Many bass live in rivers. What color crayon will you use for the bass above? Color it.

Visual Discrimination/Inference

Fish with sharp teeth are hunters. Draw a rectangle around the fish below that is **not** a hunter. What are the letters that stand for the beginning sound in this fish's name? _____

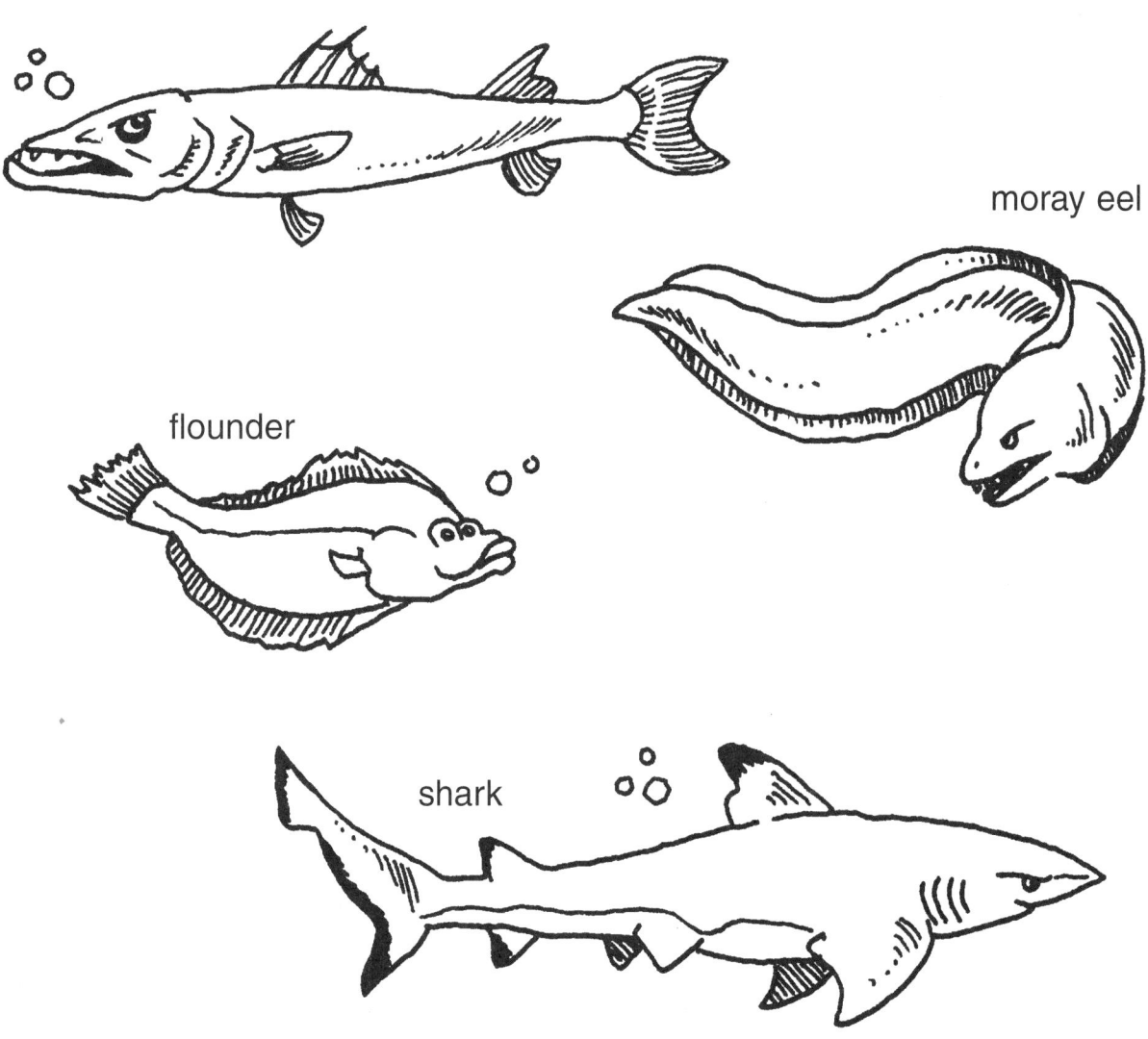

How many hunter fish do you see on this page? _____

What do you think hunter fish eat? _____
_____

Understanding Relationships/Comprehension

A lot of fish lay hundreds of eggs at a time. Most of these eggs die, but some of them hatch.

A male 🐟 keeps eggs inside a pouch until they hatch. A 🐟 makes rafts of bubbles for its eggs. A 🐟 builds a nest for its eggs. Most mother 🦈s carry their babies inside them until they are born.

Draw a line from each fish to the place it keeps its eggs until they hatch.

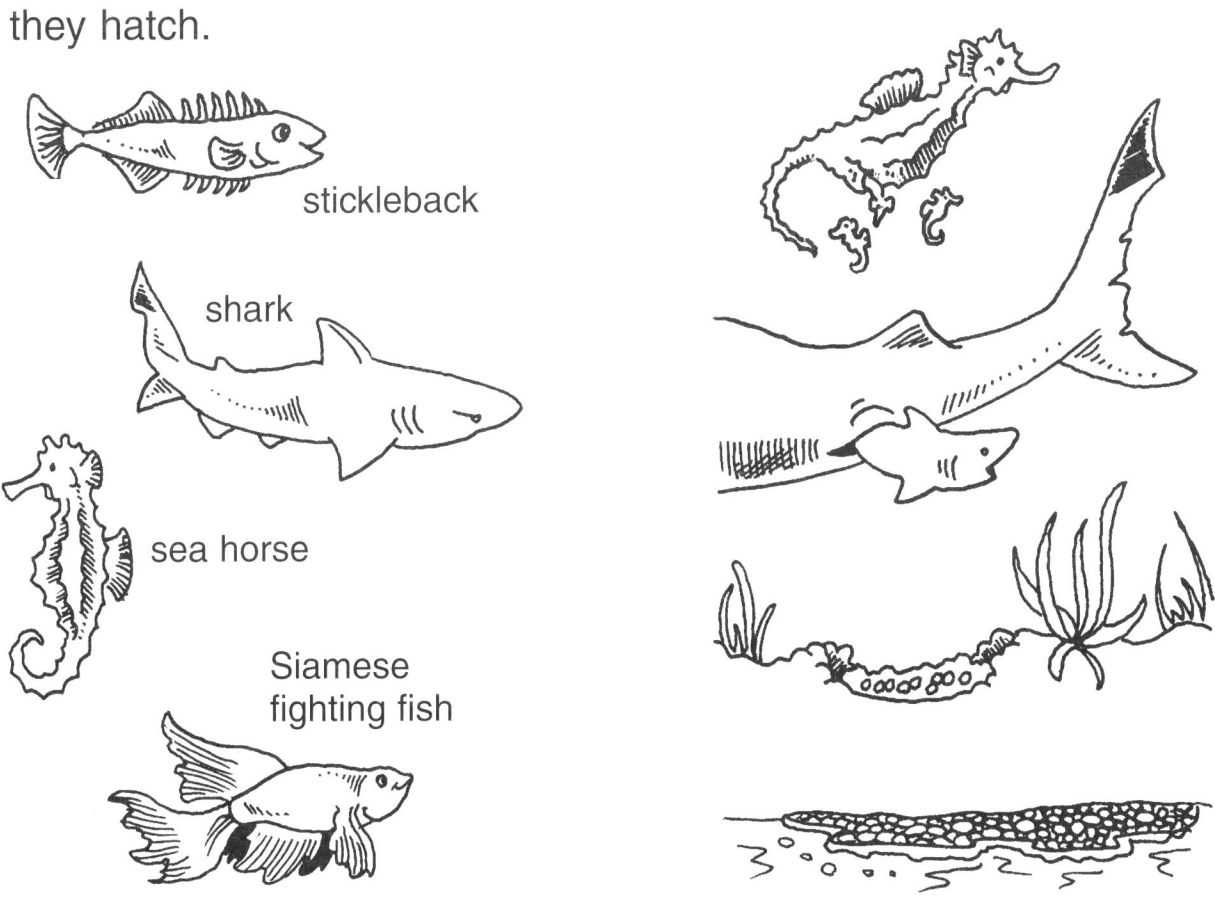

stickleback

shark

sea horse

Siamese fighting fish

Circle the father fish that carries its eggs inside a pouch.

What is the one letter that stands for the beginning sound in the names of all these fish? _____

Deduction/Understanding Relationships

Another animal family is the amphibian family. Animals in the amphibian family are alike in important ways. Frogs, toads, and salamanders are all amphibians. Newts are special smaller salamanders.

Circle one animal in each row that belongs to the amphibian family.

Amphibians do not have scales on their bodies. Most live in or near water in order to keep their skin moist, or wet, all the time. All amphibians have 4 fingers on each front foot, and almost all have 5 toes on each back foot. They do not have any claws.

Write an **R** on the reptiles below. Write an **A** on all the amphibians you see. How can you tell the difference between the reptiles and amphibians below? Explain your answer to a friend or a family member.

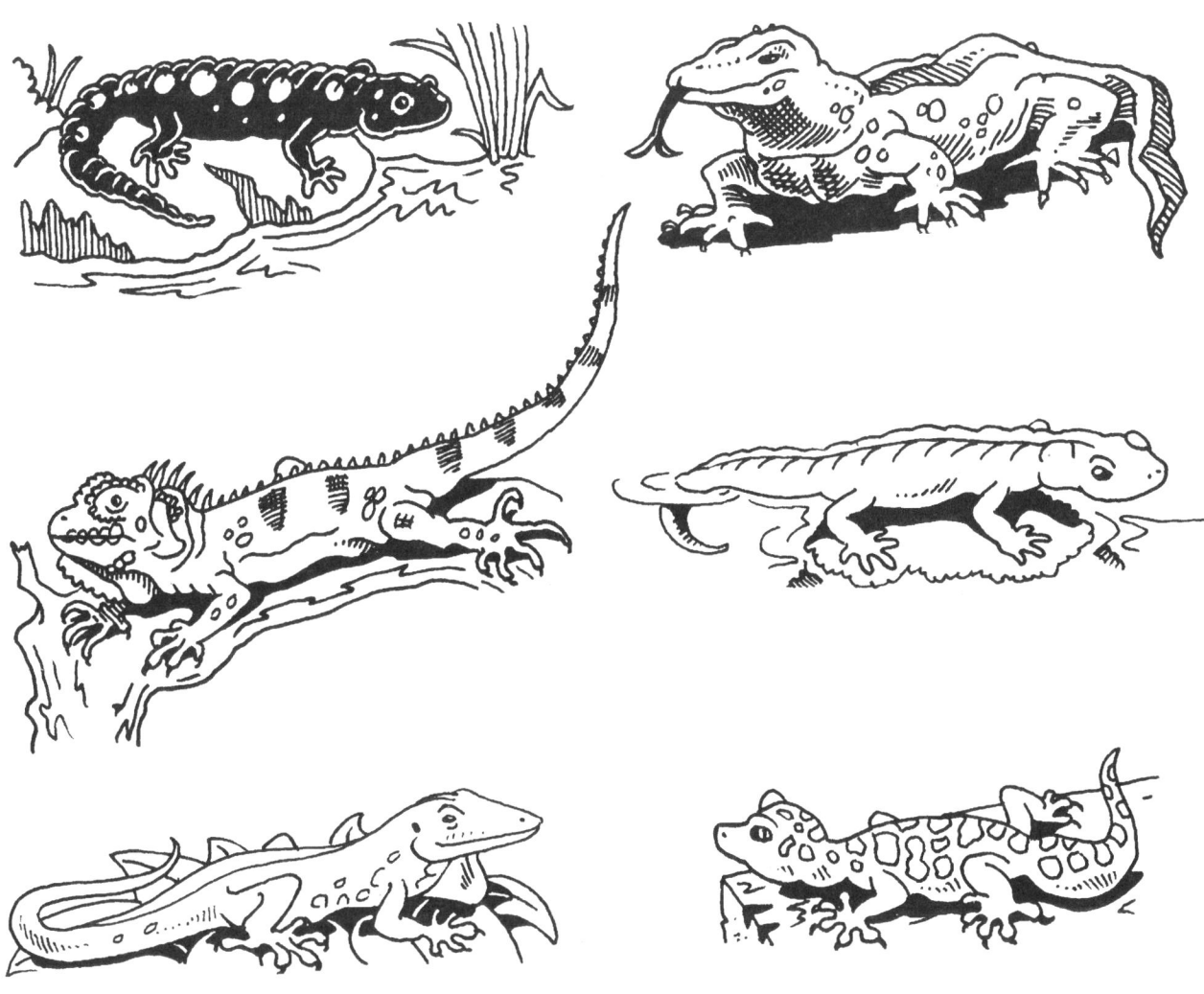

Frogs and toads are both amphibians. As adults, toads have bulging eyes and short, fat bodies with dry, warty skin. Their short legs force them to move by taking short hops. Toads mainly live on moist land. Frogs have longer, thinner legs and bodies. They have smooth, moist skin and webbed feet. Their longer legs allow them to leap, or jump, long distances. Frogs usually live in water or other wet places.

Some frogs are big. A bullfrog is bigger than your 🖐. Some frogs are small. A leopard frog can be as small as your 👉.

Inference/Deduction

Write a **T** on the toad. Circle the word that tells how toads move:
    leap   hop

Color the bullfrog green.

Draw a triangle around the frog with spots. Why do you think this frog is called a leopard frog? _____
_____

Do these frogs hop or leap? _____

Draw a rectangle around the frog's tongue. It is sticky for catching flies. Why is it long? _____
_____

Why do frogs and some toads have webbed feet?
_____
_____

Draw a square around the bulging eyes of the toad and frogs.

How do these bulging eyes help them see better? _____
_____
_____
_____

Newts and other salamanders are amphibians that have tails. Sometimes people mix up salamanders and lizards. Salamanders do not have claws or scales like lizards do.

Both newts and other salamanders have patterns on their skin. Look at the newts and larger salamanders in this picture. Then follow the directions below.

- Draw a triangle around the ringed salamander.
- Color the spots on the back of the small red-spotted newt. What color crayon will you use? _____
- Circle the salamander that has large, round spots.
- Put an **X** on the tiger salamander. Why do you think it has this name? _____

Sequencing/Understanding Relationships

How do baby amphibians grow?

Life begins when a mother amphibian, such as a frog, lays her eggs in water. A frog egg hatches into a **tadpole**. A tadpole breathes with gills like a fish. Soon legs grow. The gills disappear, and the tadpole grows lungs for breathing air. The young frog is now a land animal that looks like its frog parents.

Complete each picture story below by drawing a line from the empty box to the picture that shows the missing part of an amphibian's life.

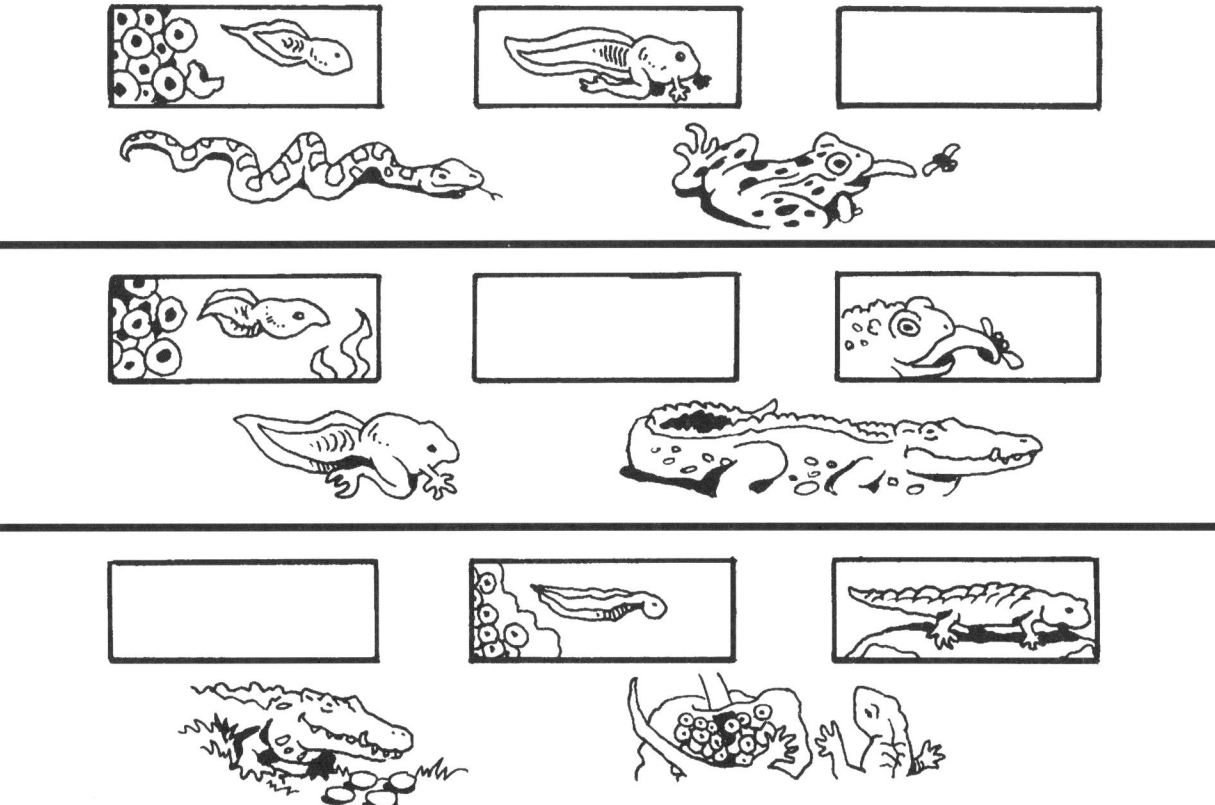

Do you know the name of another animal family? Write it here.

_____

41

Visual Discrimination/Inference

Another animal family is the insect family. Insects are usually very small. They can hide easily and can be found living almost everywhere.

Look at these insects. Decide how they are the same and how they are different. Then complete the sentences below.

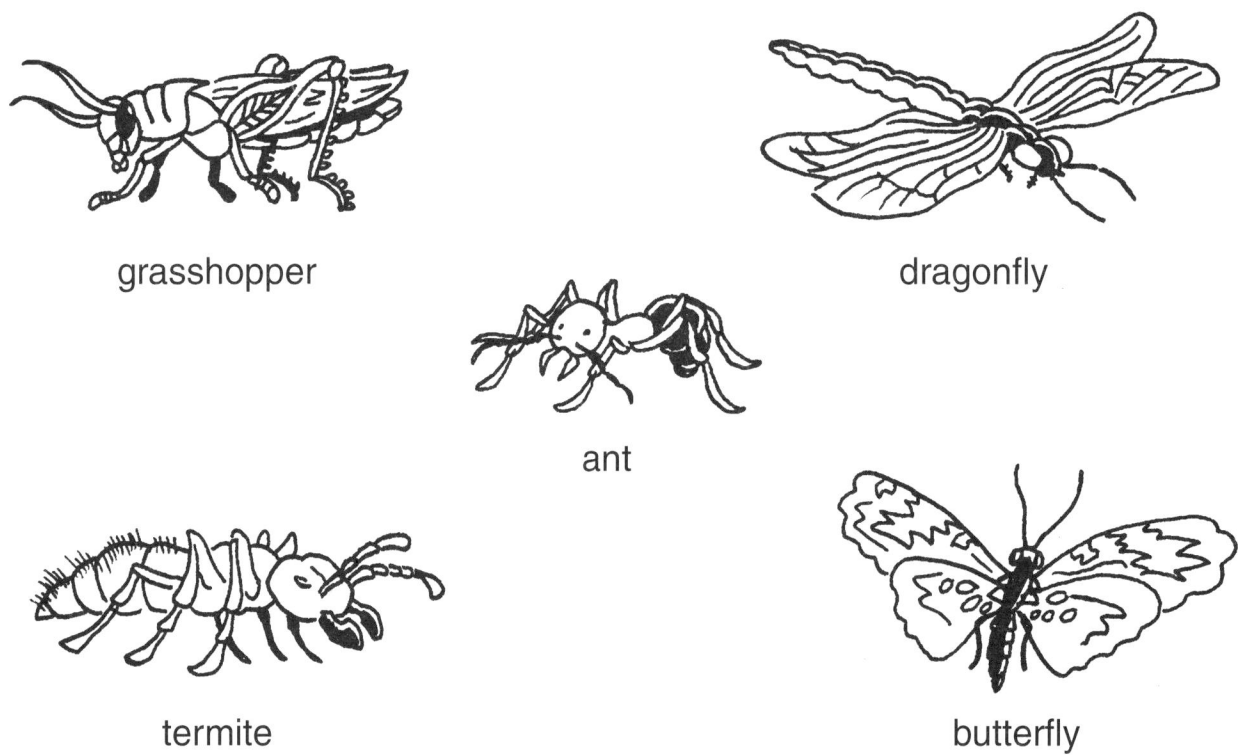

Circle the correct number in each sentence below.

   Insects have   2   4   6   legs.
   Insects have   2   3   4   feelers, called **antennae,** on top of their heads.
   The termite and ant pictured above each have   0   2   4   wings.
   The dragonfly and butterfly each have   4   5   6   wings.

Do you think insects have skin? _____

Comprehension/Sequencing

Your **skeleton** is on the inside of your body, which is covered with skin. But an insect's skeleton is on the outside of its body. It does not have skin like you do.

An insect's skeleton covers it the way a coat covers you. If your coat from last winter is too small, what would happen when you put it on? _____

When an insect grows and its skeleton becomes too small, the skeleton breaks and the insect climbs out. This is called **molting**. The insect keeps growing a new, larger skeleton until it is an adult.

What comes next? Draw a line connecting each empty box to the picture that should fill it.

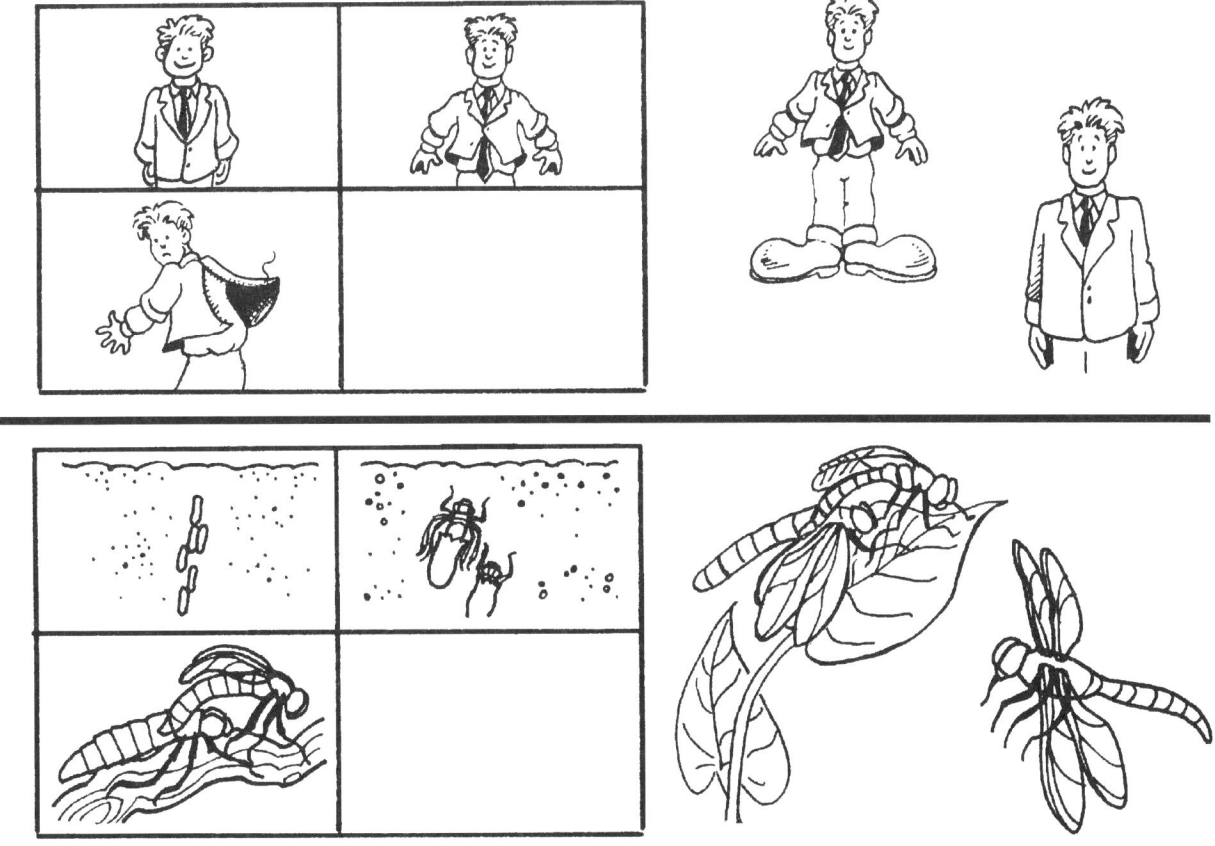

Comprehension/Sequencing

Some insects do not look like their parents when they hatch from their eggs. But, after a while, they change to look like their parents.

A mother butterfly lays eggs. Each egg hatches into a crawling caterpillar that eats leaves. Soon the caterpillar builds a **chrysalis**. Marvelous changes happen inside the chrysalis. A butterfly flies off to feed on plant nectar.

Circle the picture that answers each question below.

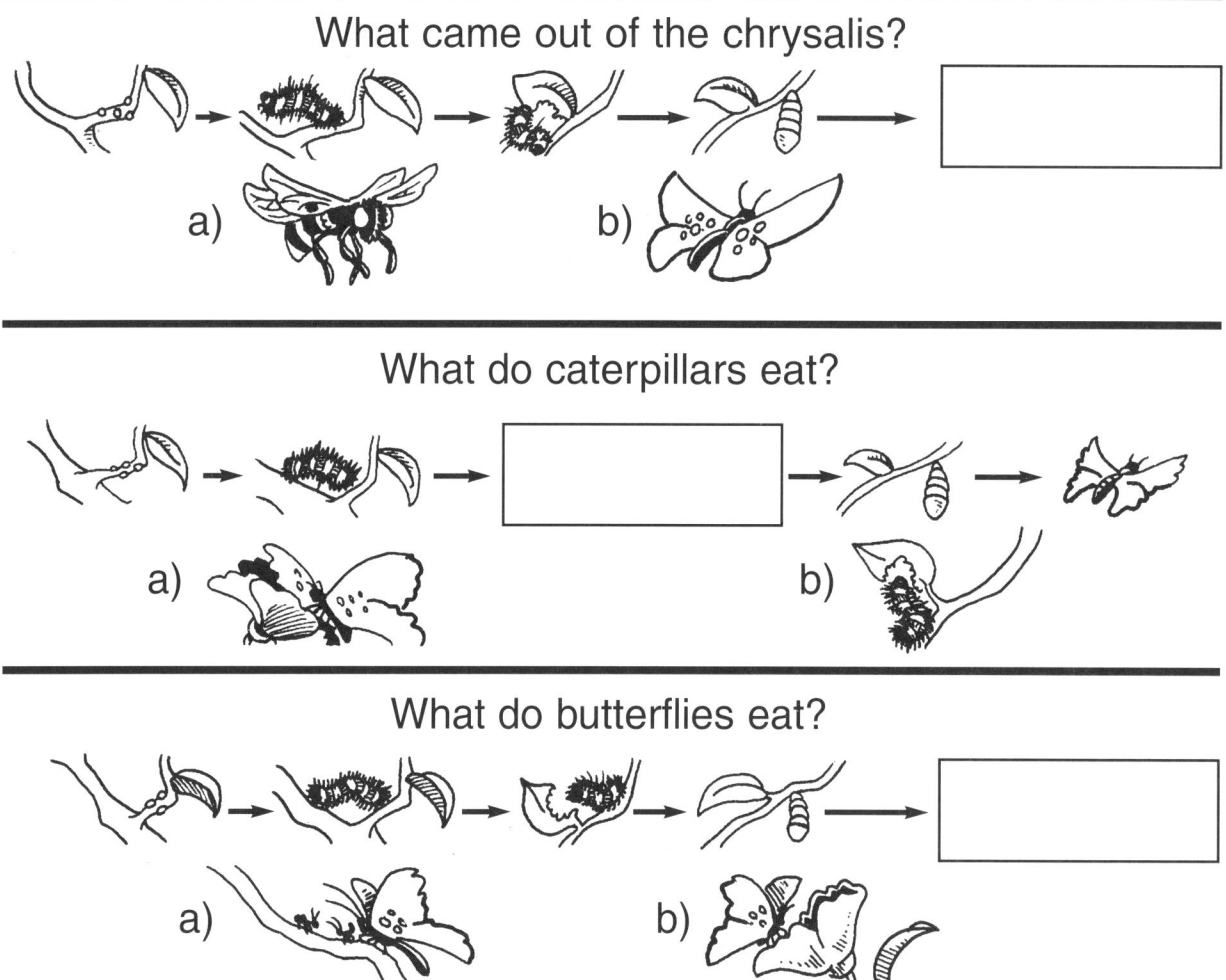

Did you know that butterflies taste with their feet?

Deduction

I am a small insect but a strong flier.
My wings make a humming sound.
I live in a **hive**.
I work together with other insects to collect flower nectar and then make honey in our hive.
What am I? _____

Use your crayons to color me yellow and black.

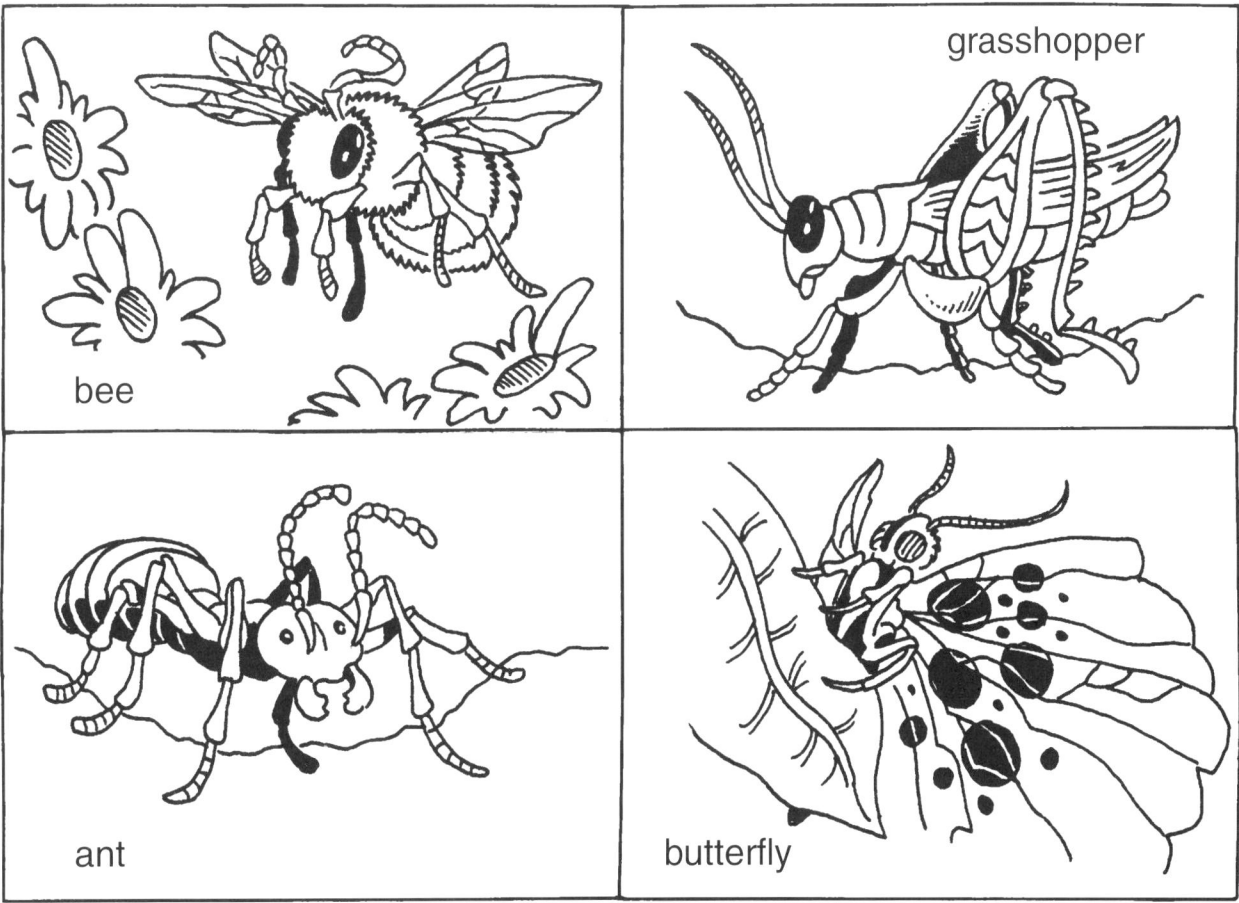

What does the insect you colored do to protect itself? _____

Comprehension/Deduction

Another family of animals is the mammal family. Animals in the mammal family are alike in important ways. They do not have fins or feathered wings or scales. Their skeletons are on the inside of their bodies.

Circle two animals in each row that are mammals.

How is a mammal's skin different from a bird's skin? _____

_____

Do some mammals have a furry coat? _____

Are you a mammal? _____

46

Mammals are covered with fur or hair. Most mammals live on land. Some mammals live in the ocean. One type of mammal can fly.

Put an **X** on the mammal in each row that is very different from all the other mammals.

How many of the mammals above live on land? _____

How many of the mammals above live in the ocean? _____

Circle the correct number in the sentence below.
    Land mammals have a total of   3   4   5   legs and/or arms.
    Ocean mammals have arms and legs that are flippers.

Analogies/Understanding Relationships

Mammals live in many different places. Polar bears, seals, and walruses are mammals that live in icy-cold places. Giraffes, lions, elephants, and zebras are mammals that live on warm, grassy plains. Black bears, deer, and monkeys are mammals that live in forests. Beavers live near rivers.

Circle the picture that best completes each sentence below.

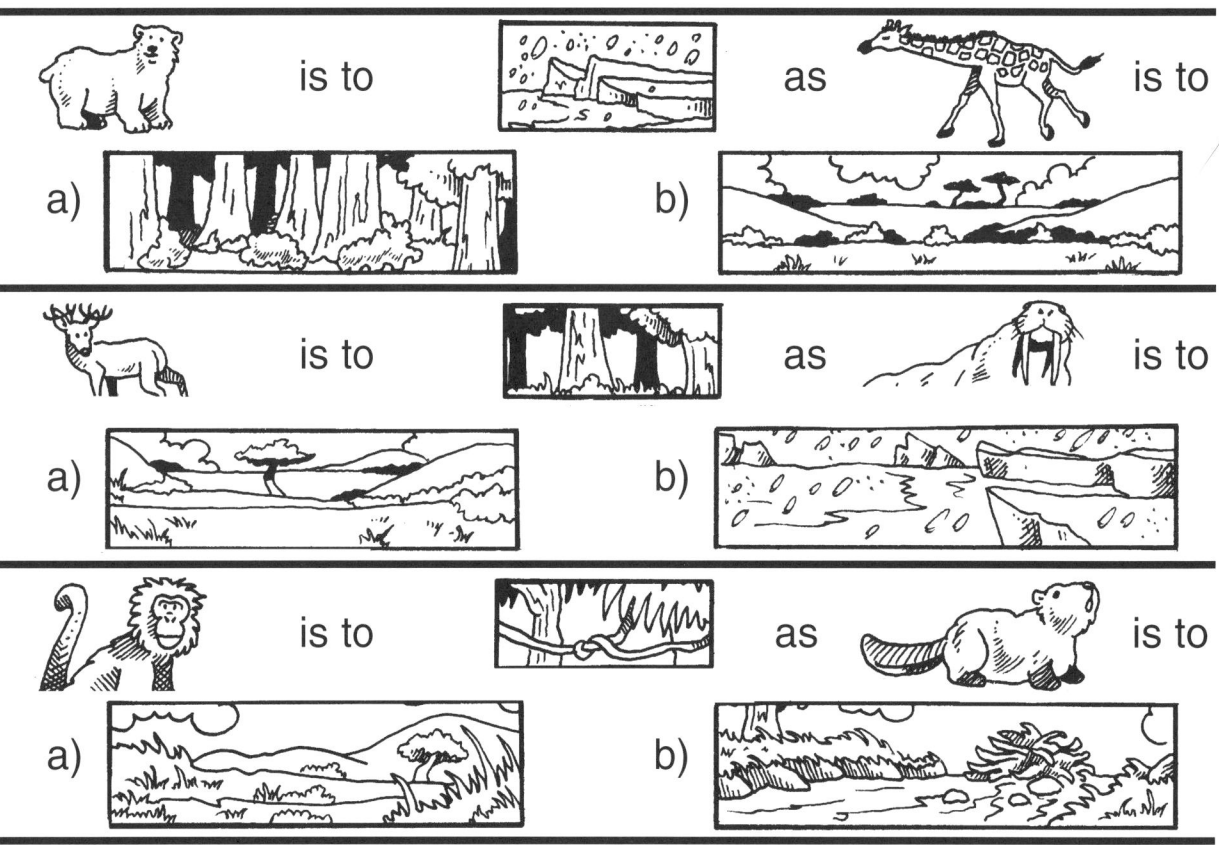

How many mammals above live in icy-cold places? _____

How many mammals above live on warm, grassy plains? _____

How many mammals above live in forests? _____

How many mammals above live near a river? _____

Inference/Understanding Relationships

Nearly all other mammals carry their babies inside them until they are born. Most baby mammals look like their parents. Mother mammals make milk to feed their young.

Draw a line from the name of each offspring to its picture.

baby human

calf

duckling

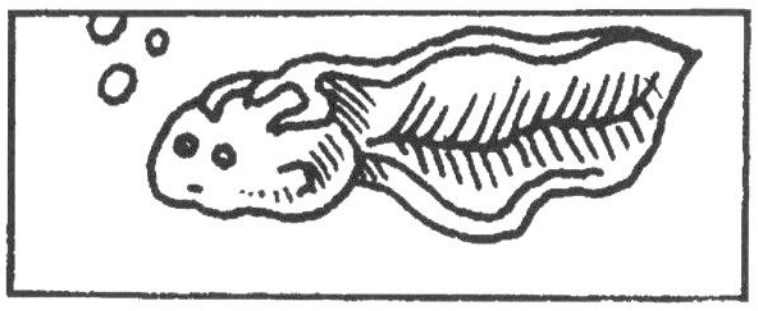

tadpole

baby turtle

How many baby mammals are pictured? _____

Say the beginning sound of each mammal's name.

49

Analogies/Understanding Relationships

Fast-running mammals with sharp teeth and claws catch and eat other animals. Slow mammals with dull teeth and **hooves** on their feet usually eat grass and other plants. Some mammals eat both plants, including vegetables and fruit, as well as meat.

Circle the picture that best completes each sentence below.

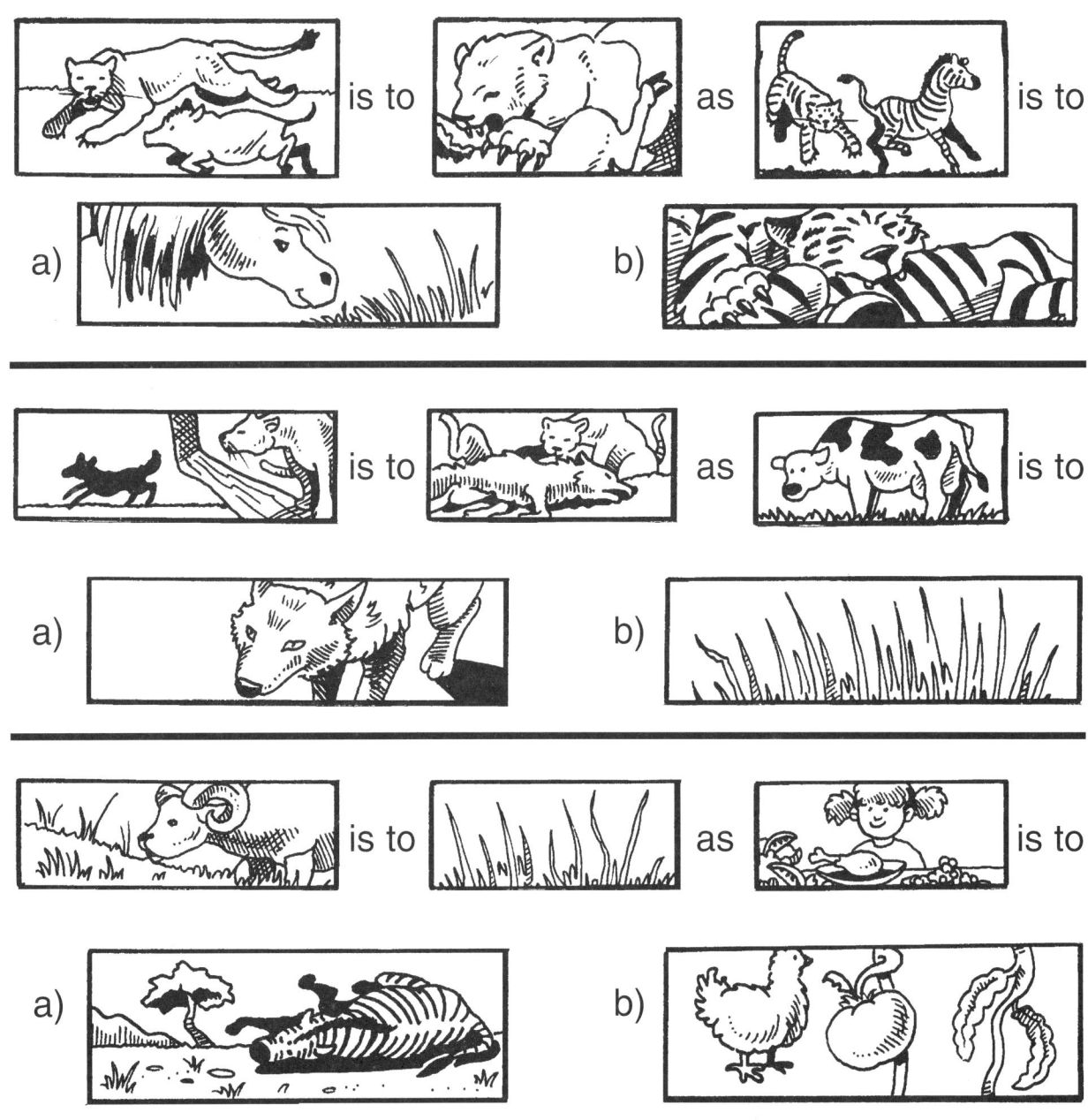

Analogies/Understanding Relationships

Some animals in the mammal family are called **primates**. They don't have hooves like cows do. They don't have claws like tigers do. They have a special kind of hand with four fingers and a thumb. Chimpanzees, gorillas, and monkeys are primates.

Circle the picture that best completes each sentence below.

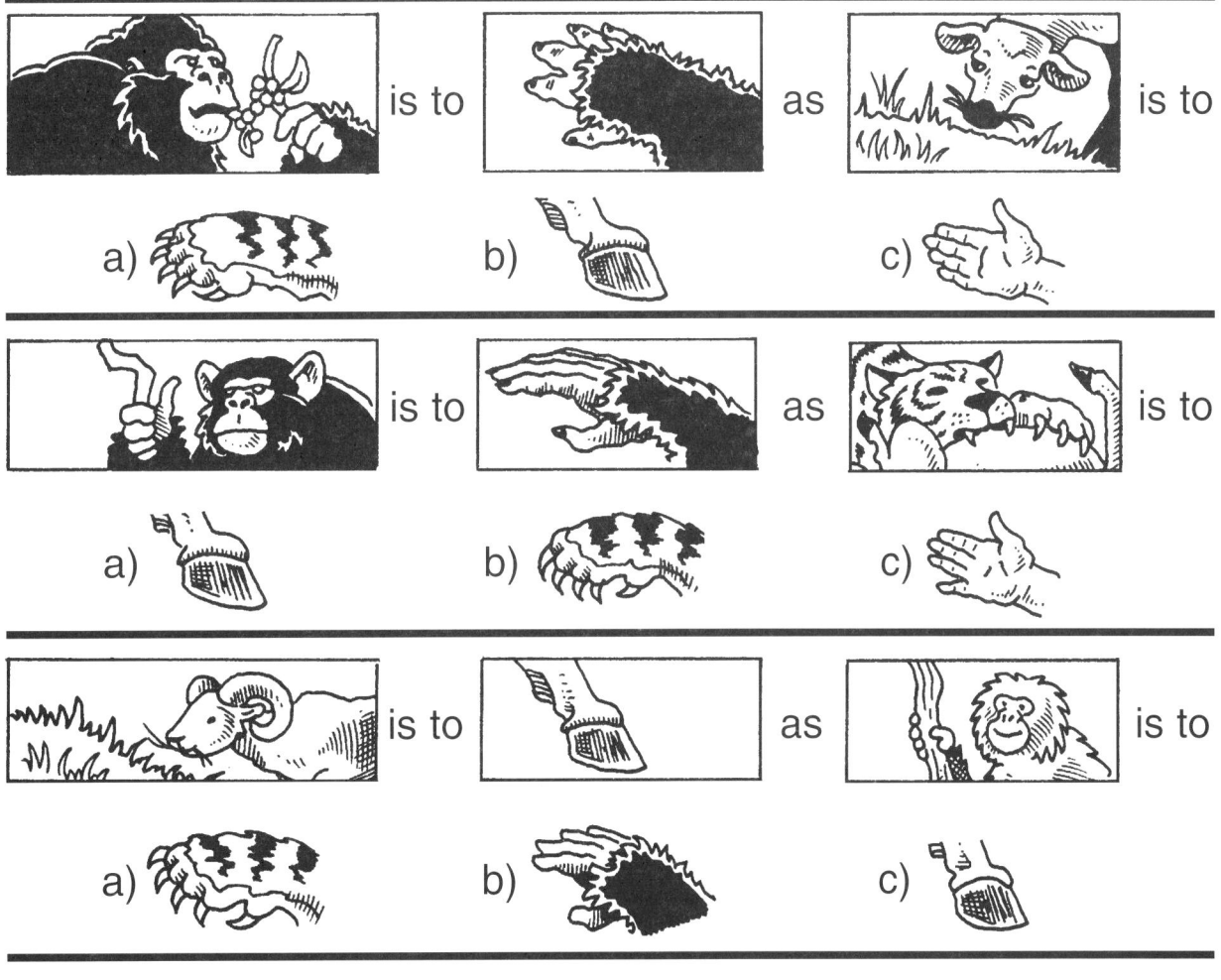

How many fingers do you have on each hand? _____

How many thumbs do you have on each hand? _____

Are you a primate? _____

Understanding Relationships/Visual Discrimination

Humans and orangutans are primates, too.

Use a crayon to draw a line from each mammal to its hand, paw, or hoof.

Why do you think primates' hands are so special? _____
_____
_____

52

Primates' hands are special because they can do things that hooves and paws cannot do. Primates' hands can hold things.

Put an **X** on the mammal in each row that **cannot** do what the others can do.

How many primates do you see on this page? _____

Deduction/Making Comparisons

Three of the four mammals in each row are alike. Circle the one that is different.

How are the other three mammals alike? _____
_____
_____

What kind of food do the other three mammals usually eat? _____
_____
_____

Making Comparisons/Creative Thinking

Look at each row of pictures below. Decide how the animals in each row are alike. Then, in the empty box, draw a picture of an animal that goes with the other animals in that row.

How are these animals alike? _____
_____
_____

What kind of animals are these? _____

Making Comparisons/Creative Thinking

Look at each row of pictures below. Decide how the animals in each row are alike. Then, in the empty box, draw a picture of an animal that goes with the other animals in that row.

How are these animals alike? _____
_____
_____

What kind of animals are these? _____

All the animals in a family are alike in important ways. Draw a line from each animal to its family house. Next to each house, write the total number of animals on this page that belong in it.

On a separate piece of paper, make a list of all the ways the animals in each family are alike.

Glossary

amphibian—Cold-blooded animal that has a backbone and spends the first part of its life in the water. All amphibians have 4 fingers on each front foot and almost all have 5 toes on each back foot.

antennae—Feelers on the top of an insect's head that smell and sense movement.

bask—To get warm by lying in the sun.

beak—See **bill**.

bill—The hard mouthpart and jaws of a bird.

birds—Animals that have feathers, two wings, a beak, and two legs. Most birds fly, but some do not.

chrysalis—The case that protects a caterpillar while it changes into a butterfly.

claws—Sharp, curved nails on the end of an animal's fingers or toes.

cold-blooded—Having a body temperature that is determined by the temperature of one's outside environment.

feathers—The soft, light outer covering of a bird.

fins—The body parts that help fish and aquatic mammals swim.

fish—Cold-blooded animals that have a backbone and no legs. Fish have gills for breathing and fins to help them swim. Many fish have coats of slimy scales.

gills—Organs for taking in oxygen from water.

hatch—To break out of an eggshell, chrysalis, or cocoon.

hive—A group, or colony, of bees; the home of a colony of bees.

hooves—Hard bony covering on the feet of some animals such as cows, horses, pigs, and sheep.

insect—A small animal that has its skeleton outside its body. All adult insects have three body parts: the head, thorax, and abdomen.

lungs—Organs in the chest of vertebrates used for breathing air.

Glossary

mammals—Warm-blooded animals that have a backbone, and fur or hair on the outside of their bodies. Mother mammals produce milk to feed their babies.

molting—Shedding or casting off an outer covering, such as skin, feathers, fur, and hair.

nectar—The sweetish liquid produced by many flowers. Bees use it for making honey.

nests—Structures that birds and some other animals make to lay their eggs in. Nests protect the eggs and the babies after they hatch.

offspring—The child of a parent.

primates—Mammals that have a special kind of hand with four fingers and one thumb that can grasp and hold objects.

reptiles—Cold-blooded animals that have a backbone and scales or bony plates on the outside of their bodies.

scales—Small, thin plates covering the outside of the body. Most reptiles and fish have scales.

shed—See **molting**.

shell—Hard outer covering, such as that of an egg or a turtle.

skeleton—The strong structure that supports or protects an animal's body.

tadpole—A young amphibian that grows up to be a frog or a toad.

webbed feet—Feet that have toes that are united by a thin layer of skin. Webbed feet help animals swim and are often found on animals that live in or near the water.

wings—The parts of a bird's, bat's, or insect's body that it uses to fly.

Answers

Page 5
Parent: Child should draw squares around the zebra, spider, fish, bird, alligator, and iguana. He or she should draw a triangle around the 6 plants.
There are 6 animals on this page.
There are 6 plants on this page.

Page 6
There are 2 animals that are birds.
There are 2 animals that are reptiles.
There are 2 animals that are fish.
There are 2 animals that are mammals.
Amphibians and insects are some other kinds of animals.

Page 7

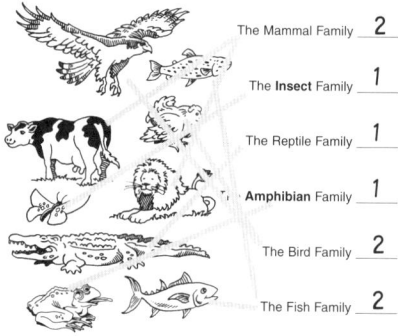

Sample answer: Animals in a family are alike in the number of legs they have, the shape of their bodies, or the kind of feet they have.

Page 8
Parent: Child should circle the picture of the parrot in the first row, the woodpecker in the second row, the seagull in the third row, and the toucan in the last row.
All birds have 2 wings.
All birds have 2 legs.

Sample answer: These birds are alike in that they all have beaks, tails, feathers, and feet, and they all build nests for their eggs.

Page 9
Parent: Child should draw a square around the heron, flamingo, ostrich, and stork.
There are 4 birds with long legs.
He or she should color 3 birds with short legs: the duck, eagle, and sparrow.
No, all the birds do not have the same kind of feet.
No, all the birds do not have claws on their feet.

Page 10

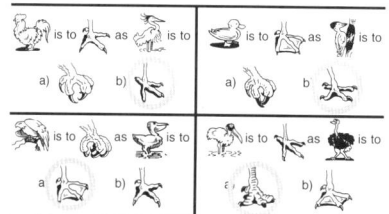

Humans have 5 toes on each foot.

Page 11

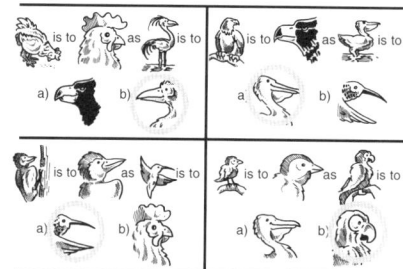

Page 12
Parent: Child should circle the picture of the eagle, woodpecker, and hummingbird in the first row; the hawk, heron, and seagull in the second row; the duck, robin, and pelican in the third row; and the owl, parrot, and peacock in the last row. He or she should have circled 12 birds altogether.

Page 13
Birds like penguins, ostriches, and emus cannot fly because their wings are too short and too weak to support them in the air.
A penguin has webbed feet to help it swim.
An ostrich has long legs to help it run very fast.

Page 14
Parent: Make sure child draws the correct body parts on each of the birds.
The top bird needs claws to hold on to the tree branch.
The middle bird needs a short, strong beak to crack seeds and nuts to eat.
The bottom bird needs wings to help it fly.

Page 15

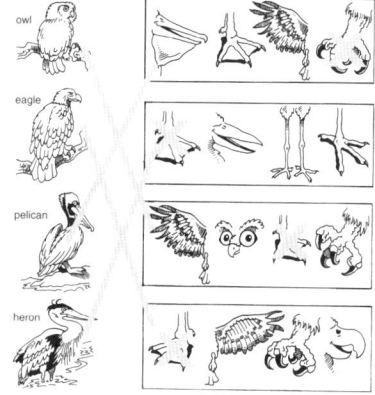

The wrong foot.

Page 16
An owl.
Parent: Make sure child colors the picture of the owl.
Owls have big eyes so they can easily see their prey at night.

Answers

Page 17

Page 18

Birds build nests so they have a safe place to lay their eggs and protect their newborn babies.

Page 19
Parent: Make sure child draws the correct pictures in the correct places.
Answers will vary but may include sticks, twigs, mud, and leaves.

Page 20

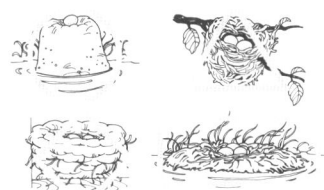

The birds use mud, grass, string, plant fibers, bark, feathers, and reeds to build nests.
Parent: Make sure child says each of these items out loud.

Page 21

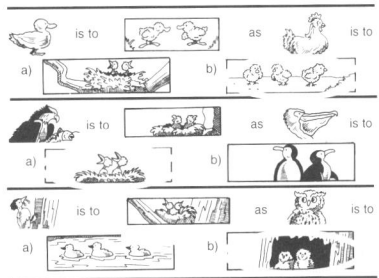

Most reptiles, and many other animals, hatch from eggs. Humans are born alive.

Page 22
Parent: Child should circle the picture of the crocodile in the first row, the alligator in the second row, the turtle in the third row, and the lizard in the last row.
Reptiles have scaly skin.
No, not all reptiles have legs.

Page 23
Parent: Make sure child draws the correct number of legs, toes, and claws on each animal. He or she should circle the alligator and the crocodile and then write **a** and **c** on the lines.
Sample answer: Reptiles are alike in that they are cold-blooded, and they all have lungs for breathing and a backbone.
Most reptiles have scales on the outside of their bodies.

Page 24
When a reptile basks in the sun, it lies in the sunshine to warm its body.
If a reptile gets too hot, it will move into the shade or water to cool off.

Page 25
Parent: Make sure child draws the snake print correctly.
Snakes shed their skin when it becomes too small for them as they are growing bigger.

Page 26
Sample answers: Ducks, penguins, and frogs have webbed feet.
Rest of answer will vary.

Page 27

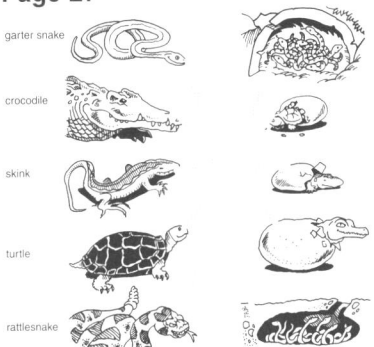

Three of the reptiles are hatched from eggs.

Page 28
Parent: Child should circle the picture of the shark in the first row, the tuna in the second row, the barracuda in the third row, and the angelfish in the last row.
A fish's skin is slimy, while a reptile's skin is dry.
No, fish do not have legs.

Page 29
Parent: Child should circle the pictures of the trout, perch, and catfish.
These fish live in freshwater rivers and lakes.
Three of the fish on this page live in salt water.
On this page, 6 fish have fins for swimming.
On this page, 6 fish have gills for breathing in water.

Page 30
Parent: Make sure child adds the correct fins to the fish.

Page 31
Parent: Child should draw a rectangle around the manta ray.
Yes, this fish has a long, thin tail.
No, the manta ray looks different

Answers

from the other fish on this page because it has large fins that look like wings, horns, and a tail.

Page 32
Parent: Child should put an **X** on the sea horse.
No, this fish is not a fast swimmer because it doesn't have a slim, streamlined body.
The sea horse got its name because its head is shaped like the head of a horse.

Page 33
Parent: Make sure child draws yellow and blue stripes on the butterfly fish.
This fish lives in coral reefs.
Child should color the tuna silvery blue.
He or she should color the bass brown.

Page 34
Parent: Child should draw a rectangle around the flounder.
The letters **fl** stand for the beginning sound of this fish's name.
There are 3 hunter fish on this page.
Hunter fish eat other fish and sea creatures.

Page 35

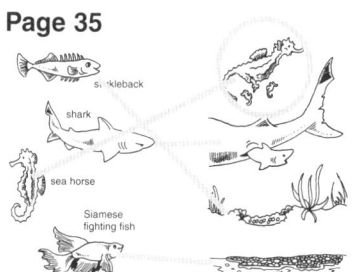

The letter **s** stands for the beginning sound of the names of all these fish.

Page 36
Parent: Child should circle the picture of the bullfrog in the first row, the toad in the second row, the salamander in the third row, and the newt in the last row.

Page 37

Rest of answer will vary.

Pages 38–39

Parent: Child should circle the word **hop**.
He or she should color the bullfrog green.
The leopard frog got its name because it has spots all over its body just like a leopard.
Frogs leap.
Frogs have long tongues so they can catch flies without moving their bodies.
They have webbed feet to help them move through the water.
Bulging eyes help toads and frogs see what is around them without having to move their bodies.

Page 40

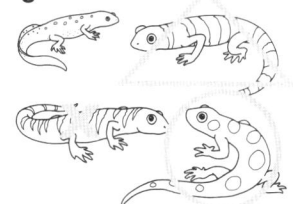

Parent: Child should color the red-spotted newt's spots red.
Tiger salamanders got their name because the stripes on their bodies look like the stripes on a tiger's body.

Page 41

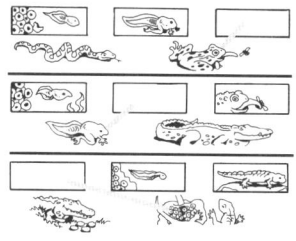

Rest of answer will vary.

Page 42
Insects have 6 legs.
Insects have 2 feelers, or antennae, on top of their heads.
The termite and ant each have 0 wings.
The dragonfly and butterfly each have 4 wings.
Insects do not have skin.

Page 43
Sample answer: A coat that is too small for you would feel tight and might even rip or tear when you put it on.

Page 44

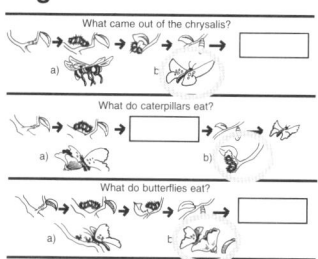

Page 45
A bee.
Parent: Make sure child colors the bee yellow and black.
A bee uses its stinger to protect itself.

Answers

Page 46
Parent: Child should circle the picture of the elephant and tiger in the first row, the lion and monkey in the second row, the dog and cat in the third row, and the whale and walrus in the last row.
Sample answer: A mammal's body is not covered with feathers as a bird's is.
Yes, some mammals have a furry coat.
Yes, humans are mammals.

Page 47
Parent: Child should put an **X** on the bat in the first row, the otter in the second row, the dolphin in the third row, and the walrus in the last row.
Ten of the mammals live on land.
Six of the mammals live in the ocean.
Land mammals have 4 legs and/or arms.

Page 48
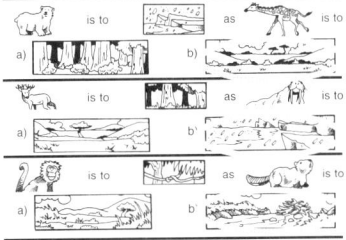

Two mammals, the polar bear and the walrus, live in icy-cold places.
One mammal, the giraffe, lives on warm, grassy plains.
Two mammals, the deer and the monkey, live in forests.
One mammal, the beaver, lives near a river.

Page 49

baby human
calf
duckling
tadpole
baby turtle

There are 2 baby mammals pictured.
The beginning sounds are **c** for calf and **b** for baby.

Page 50
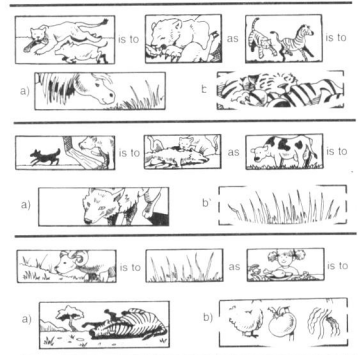

Page 51
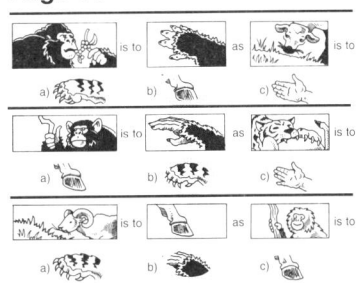

Humans have 4 fingers and 1 thumb on each hand.
Yes, humans are primates.

Page 52

Sample answer: Primates' hands are special because they can grasp and hold things.

Page 53

There are 13 primates on the page.

Page 54
Parent: Child should circle the picture of the tiger. The other 3 mammals are alike in that all are primates. Child should circle the picture of the polar bear. The other 3 mammals usually eat grass and leaves.

Page 55
Parent: Child should draw a bird in the box at the top of the page. These animals are all birds. Child should draw an amphibian in the box at the bottom of the page. These animals are all amphibians.

Page 56
Parent: Child should draw a fish in the box at the top of the page. These animals are all fish. Child should draw an insect in the box at the bottom of the page. These animals are all insects.

Page 57

Rest of answer will vary.

Other
books that will help develop your child's gifts and talents

Workbooks:
- Reading (4–6) $4.95
- Math (4–6) $4.95
- Language Arts (4–6) $4.95
- Puzzles & Games for Reading and Math (4–6) $3.95
- Puzzles & Games for Reading and Math Book Two (4–6) $4.95
- Puzzles & Games for Critical and Creative Thinking (4–6) $4.95
- Reading Book Two (4–6) $4.95
- Math Book Two (4–6) $4.95
- Phonics (4–6) $4.95
- Phonics Puzzles & Games (4–6) $4.95
- Math Puzzles & Games (4–6) $4.95
- Reading Puzzles & Games (4–6) $4.95
- Math (6–8) $3.95
- Language Arts (6–8) $4.95
- Puzzles & Games for Reading and Math (6–8) $3.95
- Puzzles & Games for Critical and Creative Thinking (6–8) $3.95
- Puzzles & Games for Reading and Math, Book Two (6–8) $3.95
- Phonics (6–8) $4.95
- Phonics Puzzles & Games (6–8) $4.95
- Reading Comprehension (6–8) $4.95

Reference Workbooks:
- Word Book (4–6) $3.95
- Almanac (6–8) $3.95
- Atlas (6–8) $3.95
- Dictionary (6–8) $3.95

Story Starters:
- My First Stories (6–8) $3.95
- Stories About Me (6–8) $3.95
- Stories About Animals (6–8) $4.95

Science Workbooks:
- The Human Body (4–6) $5.95
- Animals (4–6) $5.95

Question & Answer Books:
- The Gifted & Talented® Question & Answer Book for Ages 4–6 $5.95
- The Gifted & Talented® Question & Answer Book for Ages 6–8 $5.95
- Gifted & Talented® More Questions & Answers for Ages 4–6 $5.95
- Gifted & Talented® More Questions & Answers for Ages 6–8 $5.95
- Gifted & Talented® Still More Questions & Answers for Ages 4–6 $5.95

Drawing Books:
- Learn to Draw (6 and up) $5.95

Readers:
- Double the Trouble (6–8) $7.95
- Time for Bed (6–8) $7.95

For Parents:
- How to Develop Your Child's Gifts and Talents During the Elementary Years $11.95
- How to Develop Your Child's Gifts and Talents in Math $15.00
- How to Develop Your Child's Gifts and Talents in Reading $15.00
- How to Develop Your Child's Gifts and Talents in Vocabulary $15.00
- How to Develop Your Child's Gifts and Talents in Writing $15.00